FOR *What* IT'S *Worth*

a novel

Praise for

For What It's Worth

Reading Karey White's books, like eating chocolate cake, is always satisfying and brings a smile to my face. *For What It's Worth* is light, romantic, and delicious. It's a great pleasure read. Sit down and get lost in the charming world of wedding cakes and love.

As an added bonus, each chapter starts with a recipe, so it's a novel and cookbook all in one. A fun read!

—TERI HARMAN, KSL columnist, Studio 5 contributor, and author of *Blood Moon*, available June 22, 2013

I just loved the book—loved it. Hated putting it down and hated finishing it. Karey White is my new Maeve Binchy, her writing as warm as the bakery her novel is set in. *For What It's Worth* surprised me, made me smile, say "no" out loud in a public place. I love when a character feels like my sister. I didn't want to finish it, so now I may try the recipes that began every chapter.

—AMANDA DICKSON, author and radio personality

This book oozes charm, romance, and mouth-watering recipes. If you want to escape reality and curl up with a darling story, *For What It's Worth* is the perfect fit. Thank you, Karey White!

—RACHAEL ANDERSON, author

This is a book worth every penny of the price. In the business of baking wedding cakes, every detail must be perfection, but this story remembers that real life is oh-so-messy. White's clear and honest writing left me hungry for good food, a close family, and a little romance. A beautiful marriage of food, family, and faith.

—REGINA SIROIS, author of *On Little Wings*, 2012 Amazon Breakthrough Novel Award

KAREY WHITE

FOR 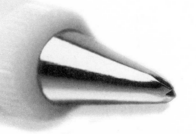 What IT'S Worth

a novel

BONNEVILLE BOOKS
An Imprint of Cedar Fort, Inc.
Springville, Utah

Also by Karey White

Gifted

No part of this book may be reproduced in any form whatsoever, whether by graphic, visual, electronic, film, microfilm, tape recording, or any other means, without prior written permission of the publisher, except in the case of brief passages embodied in critical reviews and articles.

This is a work of fiction. The characters, names, incidents, places, and dialogue are products of the author's imagination and are not to be construed as real. The views expressed within this work are the sole responsibility of the author and do not necessarily reflect the position of Cedar Fort, Inc., or any other entity.

ISBN 13: 978-1-4621-1066-7

Published by Bonneville Books, an imprint of Cedar Fort, Inc.
2373 W. 700 S., Springville, UT, 84663
Distributed by Cedar Fort, Inc., www.cedarfort.com

LIBRARY OF CONGRESS CATALOGING-IN-PUBLICATION DATA
White, Karey Lynn, 1964-
For what it's worth / Karey White.
    p. cm.
ISBN 978-1-4621-1066-7 (alk. paper)
1. Women cooks--Fiction. 2. Wedding cakes--Fiction. 3. Christian fiction. 4. Love stories.
I. Title.
PS3623.H57255F67 2012
813'.6--dc23
                            2012034849

Cover design by Erica Dixon
Cover design © 2012 by Lyle Mortimer
Edited and typeset by Melissa J. Caldwell

Printed in the United States of America

10 9 8 7 6 5 4 3 2 1

Printed on acid-free paper.

It's fitting that my first romance novel
should be dedicated to my last love.
This is for you, Travis.

One

Aunt Grace's Favorite Snickerdoodles

2¾ cups flour
2 tsp. cream of tartar
1 tsp. baking soda
Pinch of salt
2 sticks unsalted butter (soft, not melted)
1¾ cups sugar (divided use)
2 large eggs
2 Tbsp. cinnamon

Preheat the oven to 400°F.

Sift together flour, cream of tartar, baking soda, and salt; set aside. With an electric mixer, combine butter and 1½ cups sugar. Beat on medium speed until light and fluffy. Scrape down sides of bowl. Add eggs and beat to combine. Add dry ingredients and beat to combine.

In a small bowl, combine remaining ¼ cup sugar and the cinnamon. Use a cookie scoop or a small ice cream scoop to form balls of dough and roll in the cinnamon and sugar mixture. Place about 2 inches apart on cookie sheets. Bake until the cookies are set in center and begin to crack (about 10 minutes). Place the sheets to a wire rack to cool for about 5 minutes before transferring the cookies to the rack.

*T*he lawyer's office was dim and gloomy—walnut paneling, dark bookshelves filled with serious books, brown leather chairs. A gray window revealed nothing but clouds. The shadows swallowed up the weak glow of the recessed lighting and the antique lamp that sat on the corner of the desk.

A brass frog with green-jeweled eyes watched me from the shelf. It looked silly sitting there among the leather-bound books and heavy, ornate frames. A *Sesame Street* song ran through my mind. "One of these things is not like the others. One of these things just doesn't belong . . ." If Aunt Grace were here, she'd have enjoyed singing that little song with me, and we'd have laughed at the out-of-place frog.

"You doing okay, Abby?" My older brother, Evan, leaned toward me and gave my wrist a squeeze.

"I'm fine. I'll be glad when this is over."

Evan nodded.

"How is everyone today?" Gene Bellows entered the room, a short, thick man holding a thick blue folder in his thick hand. We mumbled a greeting in return. "Looks like your Aunt Grace sent you a beautiful Seattle day." He sat down at his desk, opened the file, and sorted through a few papers.

"Let's get right to this, shall we?" No one responded, but the feeling in the room was a strange mix of eager anticipation and somber sadness—Christmas and a funeral all wrapped up in one package. Mr. Bellows pulled a letter from the top of the file. "Grace asked that I read this to you before we proceed any further." He cleared his throat and then continued. "My dear family, I've lived a good life, filled with joy, laughter, and love. The greatest joy of my life has been my nieces and nephew, and with all my heart I thank you, Ellen and Rich, for sharing your children with me. I might have turned into a lonely, bitter woman, but you three children didn't give me time to feel sorry for myself. Instead, you filled my life with meaning and love. I've been so blessed and I love you all. Grace."

Mr. Bellows placed the letter behind the other papers. "All right then. Kate?" He looked from Kate to me. Kate gave a little wave, and Mr. Bellows nodded at her before he started reading. The words sounded just like Aunt Grace. "Kate. I was thinking that Izzy needs a nice swing set, and I have one in my backyard that I want you to have. It might be a little big and awkward to move, so I decided to give you the house, as well." Kate gasped. "Of course, if you don't want the house, you can move the swing set and sell the house. It's up to you and Sam, but whatever you decide, I'd like you to keep the swing set."

We all laughed. How like Aunt Grace to fill the room with her humor, even though she was gone. Of course she knew Kate would want the house. It was a charming family home on Mercer Island, just twenty minutes from where Kate's husband, Sam, was a professor of engineering at the University of Washington. It had elegant, coved ceilings, arched doorways, and rich wood trim. The yard was large and lush with big trees and mature rhododendrons.

Kate put her hands on her cheeks and looked at Mom, who smiled. "I guess you want the house?" Mr. Bellows asked, and Kate nodded enthusiastically.

"Evan." Mr. Bellows looked at Evan, who leaned forward slightly in his chair. "I know you like horses, so I think it's time you actually owned a few. And I'd imagine you'll need someplace to keep them. Remember that little ranch we drove by when I took you to North Bend for riding lessons? It's the one with the mailbox that looks like a tractor. Well, it's now yours. It needs a little work. The house is old and small, but the barn is big and solid. I think you'll do just fine there."

I had an overwhelming desire to see Aunt Grace. I couldn't help it. Evan had loved horses all his life and now this. I wanted to hug her and thank her for making his childhood dream come true. Oh, how I missed her.

"And you must be Abby," Mr. Bellows said and shifted toward me in his chair. I nodded, and he continued. "Abby, Abby, Abby. What to leave you has been a bit of a challenge for me. My plan was to find you a nice home, but even if I did, you'd still be working at that smelly tractor store. So I've done something a little different. I know you once dreamed of owning a wedding cake shop. Now you have a choice to make. I've found a place for you. The house is quite suitable. You can leave it as is, move right in, and continue working at that nasty place. But I hope you'll use the money I'm leaving you and turn it into your bakery. It's zoned for business, and you can live in the little guest house behind it."

Sweet Aunt Grace! She'd given me a house. No more rent payments.

I could get a roommate who would pay *me* rent. This could change my life. No more paycheck to paycheck. It was fantastic!

Except for one enormous thing.

The bakery.

Of course Aunt Grace knew of my dream. I'd been fourteen the first time I told her. She'd been sitting at the kitchen table grading papers while I baked a batch of her favorite cookies—snickerdoodles. They weren't my favorite cookies to make—they don't have any chocolate—but when Aunt Grace came to visit, she'd leave disappointed if she couldn't take home a little bag of "heaven rolled in cinnamon and sugar."

"So, Abby, what do you think you'd like to be when you're all grown up?"

"A mom for sure. And I want to have at least five kids." Aunt Grace nodded but didn't look up from her papers.

"Why five kids?"

"I have to have *at least* five because I have five names that I love. But mostly I want a big family because I want to be a great mom. I want to make cookies and bread and read bedtime stories and help them with their homework."

I stopped, embarrassed at my own enthusiasm. Fourteen-year-old girls aren't usually so passionate about their unborn children. "I don't know. I just really want a big family."

"I hope you have a dozen children if that's what you want." She wrote a score at the top of a paper and added a smiley face with a flourish. I thought high school students were too old for smiley faces on their papers, but that was Aunt Grace.

I lifted the warm test cookie off the cookie sheet and split it in two, giving Aunt Grace half and keeping half for myself. We each blew on our half for a moment, then raised them in the air. "Cheers," we said together and then took a bite. This was a tradition we'd started many snickerdoodle batches ago. Aunt Grace said I needed to eat at least half a cookie so I could be sure I was serving a quality treat.

"Have you thought about school or a profession?" Aunt Grace had been an English teacher for more than twenty-five years. She loved it so much, she'd kept teaching even after she'd married Jack, a wealthy businessman who died three years before Aunt Grace.

"Someday I'd like to have my own wedding cake shop." I put a pan of cookies in the oven.

"Why a wedding cake shop?"

"Can you imagine a more romantic job? I'd be baking a beautiful cake for the most important day in someone's life. It would be the best job ever."

I love romance. Nothing makes me swoon like a good love story. Elizabeth Bennett and Mr. Darcy are old friends, and by the age of fourteen, I'd lived through Scarlett and Rhett's turbulent romance three times—all 1,037 pages of it, although the third time through I skipped all the boring Ashley and Frank parts and beelined it to the Rhett parts. My favorite movie scene is in *Say Anything*. My heart turned to mush when Lloyd Dobler stood outside Diane Court's house, boombox held high above his head in a desperate effort to win her back. I still can't understand how Diane could possibly turn away and ignore a gesture that romantic? I'd have leaped out the window into his arms.

Aunt Grace sighed. "That does sound like a romantic career. And if you can make wedding cakes that are half as tasty as these cookies, you'll be famously successful." She waved the last bite of cookie through the air before popping it into her mouth.

Is it possible she knew she was foretelling the future?

Mr. Bellows's voice brought me back from my memories of Aunt Grace. "Well, young lady, it looks like you've got some big decisions to make."

"I sure do."

My 1993 Toyota wheezed to a stop at the curb. I looked at the house number on the charming bungalow. This was it. I liked it. The river rock around the base and wheat-colored clapboard siding looked warm and solid. A few houses on the street were businesses—a dressmaker and beauty shop shared a cornflower blue bungalow, and a lawyer was in a renovated Victorian, but other houses were still used as homes.

I dug the keys out of my bag and let myself in. There were several small rooms on the main floor and a large, dark basement. The kitchen was roomy but old-fashioned. The speckled linoleum floor was yellowed and cracking. It would take a lot of work to make it into a bakery kitchen, but a couple of single girls could make it work. And there were two bedrooms on the main floor, exactly what I'd need if I found a roommate.

Out the back door was a small yard. Dormant rosebushes lined the fence to the right, and an old-fashioned driveway made of two concrete strips with grass in the middle was to the left. Across the back lawn stood the small guesthouse. The key didn't seem to fit, but after a little jiggling, it finally turned. I stepped inside and felt like Alice in Rabbit's house. Everything was tiny. The front part of the house was a small room that included a kitchen and living area. And the bedroom? A large walk-in closet was more like it. Could a person really live here? I'd given up the idea of living in a playhouse at least a dozen years ago.

There wasn't room for two people here. That was certain. I'd never lived alone before, and the thought was unsettling. I liked the security of a roommate, another person in the house when I went to bed. It kept me from imagining intruders entering with every night sound I heard. Could I handle living alone? The very idea brought the music from *Psycho* to mind. I wasn't sure if I could do it. I wasn't sure if I wanted to.

"How was your date with that guy from Puyallup?" Kate asked at the monthly Benson Sunday dinner.

I swallowed a bite of salmon. "Not so good. He griped about all the pressure he feels to get married right away. I guess his bishop and his parents won't leave him alone about it. Then he pointed out what a 'babe' our waitress was and even asked me if I thought she looked too young for him. No wonder he's thirty-two and still unmarried."

"One of these days, the right one will come along," Mom said. In theory, I knew this was true, but I must admit I was getting weary of the wait. The whole dating and marriage thing had been so much easier for Mom and Kate. I, on the other hand, had dated more dead ends than I'd ever wanted to, and I was tired of the game. How on earth was I going to have a house full of kids if I couldn't even manage one good date? There had been two promising guys way back when, but they were both married now and not to me. It had been a long time since I'd dated someone I could imagine spending my life with. Maybe there weren't any great guys left.

"What have you decided to do about the bakery?" Evan asked. As the two single family members, Evan and I preferred to avoid talking about our lackluster love lives. Usually I'd have appreciated him trying to rescue me. The problem was that the bakery was also a treacherous topic, and I didn't really want to talk about that either. I was leaning toward the easy and safe roommate route, and I suspected my family would be disappointed in me. Maybe I should have faked a fever and stayed home today.

"I haven't decided for sure," I said. "Jenny Baxter mentioned at church today that she might be looking for a place to live. I think she'd be a good roommate."

"So you're not going to open the bakery?" Judging by Kate's voice, you'd have thought I was announcing my plans to free-fall off the space needle.

"Well . . ." I put a large bite of mashed potatoes in my mouth, buying a moment to prepare for the onslaught.

"Abby, you know Aunt Grace was trying to give you something that would change your life." Mom's voice carried enough reproach that I felt like a naughty six-year-old.

"I know, Mom. But a house with a room I can rent out *will* change my life." It sounded weak and I knew it.

"We need to leave it up to Abby," Dad said. I wanted to hug him, but then he continued. "Grace wanted it to be her choice, and we can't force her to do what Grace wanted." Oh! Dagger! Aunt Grace really did want me to open the bakery. I was the only one who got a house *and* the money, and she'd specified that the money was so I could get the bakery up and running. Would it be fair to take the money and not open a bakery? Maybe I could just split the money with everyone.

The dining room was silent except for the clinking of silverware and Izzy's soft and oblivious chatter from the high chair. I knew everyone was waiting for me to say something. I looked around the table. Dad, Mom, and Kate were looking directly at me. Evan and Sam were looking uncomfortably at each other.

"What?" I said.

Mom shrugged her shoulders. "I just think you should seriously consider this before you decide not to try."

"I've thought a lot about it, Mom. It feels like it's all I've thought about." I paused but no one spoke. "Why did she have to make mine hard?" I cringed. Here I was with the opportunity of a lifetime, and I was whining that it had been given to me. But I was scared. Really scared. I'd never done anything like this before, and I didn't want to fail. I'd always succeeded at everything, but part of the reason for that was because I'd never done anything truly daring.

Dad reached over and patted my hand. "Abby," he said, his voice earnest, "let me just remind you of a few things." I nodded. "I remember a fourteen-year-old girl nearly jumping out of her skin with excitement when she got home from shopping with her mom because she'd found a five-dollar cake decorating kit. And I remember that same girl making a droopy cake with daisies that looked like white spiders."

"Hey, be nice," I said.

Dad continued. "I remember those dreadful cakes becoming beautiful."

Mom jumped in. "And I remember a three-tier birthday cake that was prettier than any wedding cake I'd ever seen in my life. I was so proud of all those fondant roses, I wanted everyone I knew to see it."

"And I was so disappointed that you were on your mission when I got married," Kate said. "I almost made Sam wait a year so you could make my wedding cake."

"Sorry, Abby," Sam said, "but no cake was worth waiting that long."

"All I know," Dad said, "is that you have talent. Aunt Grace knew that. We all know it. If it doesn't work out, you can find a hundred jobs like the one you have right now. But if you don't try, you know you'll regret it." They all believed I could do it. Aunt Grace had staked a lot on that belief. Why was I so unsure? I stood up and hugged Dad.

"You know we'll help you," Mom said. I could practically see my simple life waving good-bye. I thought I might throw up.

"Of course we will," Kate said. "You'll be fine." I wasn't so sure about that. I think in order to be fine, you have to have oxygen, and right then I couldn't breathe.

Two

Cinnamon Rolls

¼ cup warm water
1½ packages dry yeast
1 cup milk
½ cup shortening
⅓ cup sugar
1½ tsp. salt
1 egg, beaten
4–5 cups sifted flour
melted butter
brown sugar
cinnamon

Add the warm water to the yeast and set aside for 10 minutes.

Scald milk. In a bowl, pour milk over the shortening. Add sugar and salt and cool to tepid. Add the dissolved yeast and beaten egg. Add flour, one cup at a time, beating after each addition.

Dough should be soft yet firm enough to handle. Knead on a floured board until elastic and smooth. Avoid too much flour. Put dough into well-oiled bowl. Let rise for 1½ hours.

Press dough down and divide into workable size. Roll dough out into a rectangle. Cover with melted butter. Sprinkle with a generous, thick layer of brown sugar (at least ¼ inch). Sprinkle with cinnamon, as desired. Roll up jelly-roll fashion.

Using scissors or a piece of string, cut off slices 1 to 1½ inches thick. Place slices into a greased pan. Press rolls down to even out and fill pan. Let rise until rolls fill the pan generously, about another hour.

Preheat oven to 350°F. Bake for 15–20 minutes.

The approval of my family has always been a deciding force in my life, so after the family dinner, I knew what I had to do. I moved my belongings to the tiny guesthouse behind my future bakery. I didn't own much—a blessing because not much would fit. I bought a small couch, and Dad and Mom gave me two stools for the kitchen counter.

I moved my cake supplies from Dad and Mom's house to my soon-to-be bakery. As I deposited the last box in the basement, I felt the first stirrings of excitement. Before long, this would be a real wedding cake bakery. I stood in the doorway to the kitchen and pictured the room after the renovations. I imagined myself at a large, stainless steel counter putting the finishing touches on a gorgeous cake. It was a sight that excited me, but too soon I felt a slow, cold chill creep up my back, and I shivered. "Stop it right now," I said aloud. "Stop being a chicken."

I hurried back to the safety of the guesthouse and did my best to replace the fear with busyness. I filled my little bookshelf with Colette Peters decorating books and *Martha Stewart Weddings* magazines.

I first found Colette Peters when I was sixteen years old. I'd been browsing the shelves at the bookstore and came across *Colette's Cakes.* The cover was a work of art—a four-tiered fondant cake that looked like silver and gold packages. I'd never seen anything like it. I sat down on the floor right there and didn't move again for almost two hours. Every picture was surprising, and the step-by-step instructions excited me like a good novel. There were cakes that looked like china, cakes with bubbles and bows and cityscapes, and cakes covered with the most exquisite handmade flowers I'd ever seen.

I hadn't had enough money to buy the book, so I'd carefully hidden it behind *The Joy of Cooking.* Two days later I made it back with the money and brought it home.

That first prized book was now joined by three more Colette Peters books and every issue of *Martha Stewart Weddings*. I'd made some variation of nearly every cake in those pages, but most had been smaller versions. It was expensive to buy all those baking supplies, and I was paying for my cake habit myself, first with babysitting money and then with money I earned working the drive-thru at a burger joint.

The bookshelf filled with all that cake experience calmed my fears. At least for a little while. At the bottom of the box was my tattered copy of *Gone with the Wind*. I put it on the shelf with the wedding cake books and magazines and made a mental note that I needed to expand my library beyond cake.

When the miniature house was bulging with my belongings, I looked around. It was comfortable and bright. The fluffy yellow and blue bed looked so cozy and comfortable, I was tempted to fall into it on the spot. The large window with small panes looked out at the back of the bakery. This would be the easiest commute of my life.

It was late, so I checked the locks on the door and closed the blinds. Here was what I'd been dreading. Late night solitude. I turned on the television to mask any unusual noises. *I can do this. I will not give up.* It would be more than a week before I'd finally go to sleep without leaving the bathroom light on and the television softly selling knives and exercise equipment from the front room.

"What comes next?" Mom asked. We were sitting in Kate's kitchen. Dad and Mom were there to install a new dishwasher. I was there because Kate had mentioned on the phone that she was making cinnamon rolls.

"Honestly, I don't even know where to start," I said. A fresh wave of freaked-out panic swept over me. I'd been pummeled by these waves for several days now. "What do you think I should do first?"

"I think you need to find a contractor." Dad said. "You remember Jim Shaw? He and Jan just had their kitchen remodeled. A real high-tech remodel with a huge refrigerator and a fancy commercial oven. I thought about you when I saw it, so I wrote down the name of his contractor." He pulled out his wallet and handed me a folded piece of paper.

"Thanks, Dad."

"You still need to think of a name," Kate said as she tried to feed Izzy another bite of applesauce.

"The name you choose might influence what the shop looks like," Dad said.

"Do you have any ideas for a name?" Mom asked.

"Not yet."

"Let's think of one right now." Mom sounded excited. She loved a good brainstorming session.

"How about 'The Cake Lady?' " Dad said.

"Abby's Cakes," said Kate.

"Emerald City Cakes."

"Sugar and Spice."

"West Seattle Cakery."

"Aunt Grace's Wedding Cakes."

"I want cake," Izzy said and we laughed.

I wanted something clever and catchy, and so far, nothing excited me.

"Miss Benson's Cakes," Mom said.

"Miss Benson's Delicious Wedding Cakes," said Dad.

"Miss Benson's Delicious and Delightful Wedding Cakes," said Mom.

"I've got it," Kate said with a smirk. "Miss Benson's Delicious and Delightful Wedding Cake Treasures." She even said it with a really bad British accent.

"Please, stop," I said. "I don't know what I want the name to be, but that wouldn't even fit on a sign."

"You could write small," Kate said.

The room was quiet for a minute as everyone tried to think of a fitting name. "Why is it so hard to think of a good name?" I asked. "Running the bakery is the hard part. Choosing a name should be a piece of cake."

"Are you kidding, Abby?" Kate said after a few seconds.

"Kidding about what?" I asked.

"That's perfect." Kate started laughing.

"What's perfect?" Mom asked.

"A piece of cake," she said and looked at each of us. "A Piece of Cake. That's a great name."

I thought a moment and nodded slowly, repeating the words. "A Piece of Cake."

"What do you think? Do you like it?" she asked.

"I do like it. In fact, I love it," I said.

"That would put you in the front of the phone listings," Dad said. That's just the sort of advantage Dad would notice. Sometimes it surprised me how quickly he saw something the rest of us hadn't even thought of.

Mom clapped and Kate and I gave each other a high five. Izzy, wanting in on the celebration, started pounding the high chair tray. It was a good name—simple, but catchy. The bakery had a name. I was thrilled!

That evening, I pulled on some warm pajamas and pink fuzzy socks and thought more about the bakery's new name. I looked at the back of my shop. The stretch of yard between the guesthouse and the bakery looked neat and pretty in the cold, January twilight. Stepping stones led from my front step to the back steps of the shop, about thirty feet away. "What do you think of your new name?" I asked the bakery and then laughed.

My silliness was interrupted by the ringing of the telephone.

"Hi, Abby. This is Jerry." I closed my eyes as I fell onto the couch, recalling his loud laugh, darting eyes, and toothy grin. After our dreary date, I hadn't expected to hear from him again. Why would he want to repeat such an unpleasant experience? Immediately I thought of excuses that would prevent a second misspent evening.

"Hi, Jerry," I said. It was difficult to muster up some enthusiasm.

"I'm embarrassed to be calling you, but I have an awkward question and I decided, what the heck, I'll just give it a shot." He laughed loudly although neither of us had said anything funny.

I squeezed my eyes shut and held my breath.

"You know the waitress the other night?" My eyes flew open.

"Yes, I remember," I said, recovering from the shock and insult of what appeared to be coming.

"You didn't happen to notice her name did you, because I called the restaurant and they have two waitresses that fit my description, and they didn't know which one it was. I'd like to give her a call, but I didn't see her name."

Of course you didn't. I slowly shook my head, remembering how he'd looked the waitress up and down. Then, feeling compassion for the poor, young waitress named Angie, I said, "Wow, Jerry, I wish I'd have paid more attention. I'm sure I would have if I'd known you were going to be tracking her down. So sorry."

"Oh what the heck, it was worth a shot." He laughed again. Could he really not hear the disgust in my voice? "I guess I'll just have to go back to the restaurant and hope I run into her."

"Yeah, I guess you will. Good luck with that." Bad dates and inappropriate guys bring out the worst in me.

"Alright-y then, Abs. Thanks anyway."

Abs? Really? I clicked the end button and laughed, amazed at the audacity. I should have felt only relief that he wasn't calling to ask me out again, but part of me was miffed that he'd call me back without showing the least bit of interest in *me*. It was an irrational reaction, but my ego didn't need to be knocked around by someone like Jerry. I glanced at the clock and was disappointed to see it was too late to call Kate and share this shameful slight. Instead I made myself a cup of hot cocoa and curled up on my couch with a calendar and my notebook.

Lists are a particular talent of mine. I've been good at them since I was a kid. I usually have two or three lists going at a time. Most people make grocery lists or to-do lists, but my list skills go much further than that. I have lists of movies I want to see, books I want to read, names I like, goals I have, favorite wedding websites, and more. I keep my list notebook in my purse, so it's there whenever I need it. My lists help me feel motivated and in control. It gives me a little thrill to put a line through each finished task and then look back to see how much I've accomplished. And now it was time to give myself a little clarity by making a bakery to-do list.

In just a few minutes, I'd filled more than a page with things that needed to be done. At the top of the list was setting a date to open the shop. A date would help keep me focused and moving forward. I thumbed through the calendar and studied each month, hoping for inspiration. Today was January 8. How soon could everything be ready? My list looked daunting.

Hire the contractor.
Order a sign.
Decide on decor.
Buy a business license.
Purchase supplies.
Shop for appliances.
Make a price list.
Print business cards and brochures.
Make dummy cakes for display.
Get a listing in the phone book.
Check on advertising rates.
Research wedding fairs.
Get a vehicle for deliveries.
Quit my job at Harward Heavy Equipment.

There was so much to do. How soon could these things be done? Valentine's Day would be romantic, but that was much too soon. There wasn't a day that excited me in March. April Fools Day was probably a foolish idea. April 28 was Aunt Grace's birthday. Could the bakery be finished by then? Could I be ready? It seemed like a fitting day to open—a tribute to Aunt Grace, who had made this whole thing possible. I circled the day on the calendar and wrote in big letters across the square, "OPENING DAY!!!"

I closed the calendar and the notebook with a new sense of determination. April 28. A little less than four months away.

That night, sleep was elusive. I got up twice to add something to my list and finally put the notebook and a pen on the floor by the bed. With my eyes closed and an infomercial about 1980s power ballads playing at low volume in the background, I pictured myself delivering a wedding cake to a beautiful backyard. A table was set up in a white gazebo, and a breeze was lightly blowing the gauzy tablecloth. In the distance, Puget Sound rippled and sparkled. The cake was four tiers covered with calla lilies that I'd made myself. It looked like something out of a dream. And maybe it was, because it was about then that I fell asleep.

Three

Basic Buttercream

1 cup salted butter (room temperature)
1 Tbsp. vanilla
4 cups powdered sugar
4–5 Tbsp. cream

Whip butter and vanilla until light and fluffy. Add powdered sugar a little at a time. Be careful of flying powdered sugar. Add cream and whip.

"Harward Heavy Equipment, this is Abby, can I help you? . . . Just a moment please." I transferred the call to Mr. Lynch. There was nothing romantic, sweet, or charming about Harward Heavy Equipment. The place looked, sounded, and smelled like heavy-duty, hard-working men. The noise of heavy machinery burst into the lobby whenever a door was opened, and the smell of oil and grease hung heavily in the air. It was a challenge to even *think* romantic wedding cake thoughts in a place like Harward, but I tried.

I pulled out the piece of paper Dad had given me and laid it on the desk. Reynolds & Sons Construction. From the bottom drawer of my desk, I retrieved the phone book, hoping Reynolds & Sons had a listing. I flipped through the yellow pages and there it was—a quarter-page advertisement that said there was no job too large or too small. They handled residential and commercial remodels (that was good news) and specialized in restoration. They were honest, hardworking, and attractive. At least the smiling man with the tool belt was. I punched a button to get a new line and dialed the number.

"Reynolds & Sons," a female voice said.

"Hi, I need to get a quote on a remodel job. I'm turning a little bungalow into a . . ." I was interrupted by the phone ringing. "Could you hold on one second?"

"Sure."

"Harward Heavy Equipment, this is Abby, can I help you? Just a moment please." I transferred the call, but before I could pick up my Reynolds and Sons call, line three began flashing and ringing. I answered the call and transferred it to the Sales Department. Then I pushed the button for my call again. "Hello? Are you still there?"

"I'm here," said the friendly voice. "How can I help you?"

"Yes, I need to visit with someone about a remodeling job I have. I need to change a home to a bakery, and I'm on a pretty tight schedule." Line three rang again. "I'm sorry. Could you hold on again?"

"Of course," she said.

As I transferred the call, another call rang in. This wasn't going well, and I felt frazzled. A minute later, I picked up my call. "I am so sorry. I think I'm going to have to call you back during my lunch. Things just got really busy here."

"I understand." I was glad she still sounded pleasant. Another line rang before I'd even hung up.

I suddenly realized that if I wanted to open my bakery, I couldn't work here. How could I get everything on my list done *there* while I was answering phones and filing away invoices *here?*

My mood matched the dismal Seattle weather on the other side of the plate glass windows. Big drops of slow rain polka-dotted the sidewalk. Aunt Grace had left me enough money to remodel the house and live comfortably for a year. I didn't need to transfer phone calls to schedule backhoe repairs. I needed to work on my bakery. I needed to treat this opportunity like a real career and give it my full-time attention.

Between phone calls, I pulled out a piece of paper and wrote "pros" and "cons" at the top of the sheet. I had to think this through. On the "pro" side I listed all the reasons why I should devote myself full-time to the bakery. Then I turned my attention to the cons. A few minutes later, the column was still empty. Something stirred up my insides until they hurt, but I knew what I had to do. I wiped my sweaty palms on my skirt, whispered a quiet prayer, and walked into Mr. Lynch's office. Ten minutes later, I'd quit my job.

❧

Dane Reynolds, of Reynolds & Sons Construction, was meeting me at 7:30 Wednesday morning. I woke up at 7:20 and threw on some gray sweatpants and a faded yellow, long-sleeved T-shirt. When I opened the front door of my cottage, a frigid blast of air sent me back inside for a warm, bulky sweatshirt. I hurried across the yard to the bakery, eager to be out of the cold wind that whipped my hair into my eyes and mouth. I opened the back door and immediately heard the sound of knocking on the front door. I looked at my watch. 7:28. *That's good. They're punctual.* I've always hated waiting on people.

"Hi," I said, opening the door.

"Hi," the man said back. It was almost like a scene from a movie. The girl opens the door. The tall boy is on the front steps, silhouetted against the morning sky. He's incredibly handsome, and there's an immediate attraction. The boy looks tenderly at the lovely girl who opened the door.

Oh crap. The girl opening the door didn't look lovely at all. She was standing there in a big, ratty sweatshirt, her hair an unruly mess, and she hadn't even brushed the morning yuck from her teeth. I immediately regretted my lack of morning preparation. I reached up and tried to smooth out my hair. If only I'd known I was about to meet a gorgeous, single man.

Yes, he was single. His left hand was holding a clipboard and with only a slight adjustment, I was able to see his ring finger, and it was gloriously empty. I learned a long time ago to check the ring finger before I check out the face. Why get excited about a face if that face is unavailable?

"Am I at the right place?" he asked.

"Mm-hmm," I said, stupidly looking up at him.

"Can I come in?"

"Oh, of course." I felt silly and sloppy and self-conscious as I stepped out of the way. "This is it," I said with a sweeping gesture of my arm. "There's a lot to be done." He stepped inside and I instinctively took a few steps back. I didn't want to assault him with my morning breath.

"Let's take a look around." He had a deep voice, and I could picture him singing bass. It looked like he might be smiling a little, and I hoped he wasn't secretly laughing at my bedraggled appearance. He pulled a pen from the top of the clipboard and flipped over a paper. "Oh, I'm Dane, by the way," he said as he shifted the pen to his left hand and put out his right hand.

"I'm Abby." His handshake was big and firm. His hand wasn't rough, but it wasn't too smooth either. I liked that. It felt like a man's hand should feel. I was surprised at how warm it was since he'd just come in from the cold, and I felt an absurd disappointment when he took his hand back.

"So what are your plans here?" he asked.

"I'm converting this place to a bakery. I'll be making wedding cakes." I described the changes I'd need as we walked through each room. We talked about appliances and windows. He tapped the wall between the dining room and the living room to see if it could come down. In the basement, Dane took some measurements while I talked. "I'll have some storage in the kitchen, but I'll need shelves built down here that can hold a variety of cake stands and other supplies. If it works to take down the wall between the kitchen and one of the bedrooms, I'd like to do that so there's plenty of workspace. The other bedroom can be turned into an office, but it will probably need to have some work done so it's wired for a phone and computer."

I realized I was talking way too fast. I do that when I'm nervous. I stopped talking, followed him back upstairs, and waited as he walked around the rooms. He measured, tapped on walls, checked out the wiring, and looked at pipes.

"How did you find out about us?" Dane asked from under the sink.

"My dad got your name from Jim Shaw. I think you did his kitchen."

"Oh, Jim. That was a great kitchen. Does your dad work with Jim?"

"They go to church together."

Dane pulled himself out from under the sink and looked at me. "Are you LDS?" he asked.

"I am."

"Me too." Had I just won the lottery? No ring *and* he was LDS. This day couldn't get any better. Then I remembered how I looked.

He asked a few more questions about the renovation and wrote down some notes. After our tour, he leaned back against the old kitchen counter with one foot casually hooked over the other. He explained the building permits we'd need, asked a few more questions, and wrote more notes.

I've been around good-looking guys before. I usually handle myself appropriately and don't make a fool of myself, but for some reason, I couldn't keep my eyes off this one. I tried to distract myself by studying the light fixture and counting the electrical outlets, but there was nothing else in the room that could hold my gaze. He was at least six-foot-two, maybe six-foot-three. His light brown hair had a little curl at the ends that brushed his ears and collar. His olive green eyes matched his long-sleeved T-shirt. They wrinkled a little at the corners as he studied the paperwork he was working on. They did the same thing when he smiled.

He moved to the little room off the kitchen and stood there looking at it for a few moments. His profile looked like a billboard for Gillette. There was no scruff on his chin, which told me he'd shaved that morning. I couldn't say why, but that pleased me. I was wondering if he shaved every morning when his voice jolted me back to the kitchen. "So, you said you're in a hurry. What's your time frame?" he asked. He looked directly at me and for a second I couldn't remember what we were talking about.

"Excuse me?"

"When do you need this to be finished?"

"Oh. Right. I'd like to open on April 28?"

Dane whistled. "That soon, huh?"

"I know it's fast, but that's my Aunt Grace's birthday, and since this is all happening because of her, I thought it would be nice to open the shop on her birthday. I'd need to have a week or two to get moved in and set up." I paused, trying to read his expression. "That's really fast, isn't it?" I tried to hide my disappointment. He looked up from his notes and scanned the room again. Then he looked at me for several seconds. I could feel the color rising in my cheeks, and I looked down at my hands.

"Well, it'll be close, but I think it's possible. If we time it right with permits and inspections, I think we can do it." I smiled. "But we need to get started right away. Let me go over these numbers with my dad and I can give you a quote this afternoon. Will you be around if I stop back by at one?"

"Definitely," I said. "Thanks." I closed the front door behind him and then stepped over to the window and watched him leave. He covered the distance to his truck in just a few strides. He tossed his clipboard onto the passenger seat as he climbed in and left without looking back. In those brief moments I made my decision. It would take a pretty shocking quote to prevent me from hiring Reynolds & Sons. The prospect of Dane Reynolds working on my bakery for the next three months had my heart doing an embarrassing little happy dance.

You can be certain that I was cleaned up, presentable, and sweet-smelling when Dane came back in the afternoon. I'd carefully picked out a faded pair of jeans and a pumpkin-colored turtleneck sweater that I thought looked good with my wavy auburn hair, brown eyes, and smattering of freckles. My two-inch heeled boots made me look a little taller than my five feet four inches, and I'd pulled my hair into a high, casual ponytail that showed off the cheekbones Mom said were my best feature. And I'd brushed my teeth. Twice. I thought I looked casual and put together, maybe even a little pretty.

Dane didn't catcall or tell me I was a sight for sore eyes, but I caught him glancing at me several times during our little discussion of details. We agreed on a price and signed the contract. I gave him a key, and we were finished. He wanted to make our deadline, so he was going to get the permits started that very afternoon. I was happy with the deal we'd struck and felt more excitement than I'd expected, but inside I knew that at least part of my enthusiasm had something to do with the "& Sons" portion of Reynolds & Sons.

I stood at the window and watched Dane leave for the second time that day. The difference was that this time he looked back at me and smiled before he climbed in his truck and was gone.

Four

Pumpkin Mini Chocolate Chip Muffins

¼ cup soft butter or margarine
1 cup sugar
1 cup fresh or canned pumpkin
2 eggs
3½ cups flour (divided use)
4 tsp. baking powder
½ tsp. cinnamon
½ tsp. nutmeg
½ tsp. salt
1¼ cups 2 percent milk
1 cup mini chocolate chips

Preheat oven to 400°F. Put muffin cups into muffin tins or grease the tins.

Cream butter (or margarine) and sugar until fluffy. Beat in pumpkin and eggs. Dredge chocolate chips in ½ cup of flour. Sift remaining flour and cinnamon, nutmeg, and salt together. Pour milk into mixing bowl. Stir in dry ingredients by hand until just mixed. Fold in the chocolate chips. Spoon batter into paper cups in muffin tin.

Bake for 20–25 minutes.

*T*wo days after the contract was signed, Dane Reynolds knocked on my door just before eight in the morning. He and two of his men were beginning demolition on the bakery, and he didn't want the noise to alarm me.

I stopped by to check out the progress as often as I dared. Dane always stopped what he was doing to give me a little tour. Once in awhile, he'd knock on my door with a question. It was exciting to see the progress, and of course it was a nice bonus that it gave me opportunities to see Dane.

My notebook filled up with more lists—things to do, things to purchase, cake designs. I almost needed a list to keep track of my lists. I opened to the first to-do list and looked it over. It made me feel satisfied to see lines through several of the items.

One afternoon, I sat on the couch and browsed the Internet, gathering information about bridal shows. Before long I was booked into the Pacific Northwest's largest bridal fair at the Washington State Convention and Trade Center. It seemed strange to be booking something for October. That seemed so far away. But weddings were usually planned well in advance. I'd have to get used to planning ahead.

"What's the latest?" Kate asked. She called almost daily for bakery updates.

"I bought six Styrofoam dummy cakes. James even gave me a fifty-percent-off coupon for the biggest one because I've been there so much."

"James? You're on a first-name basis with him?" James was the owner of Westco-Bakemark, the store I now frequented more than any other.

"What do you expect? I've been there three times in the last week."

"Is James cute?" Kate asked.

"He's as cute as any sixty-year-old I've ever seen," I said. "I'm especially fond of his diamond studs. Very attractive."

Kate laughed. "Sounds very Harrison Ford-ish."

"Poor Harrison. He lost any chance with me when he got his ears pierced. So did James."

"My, aren't you picky."

"I'd like to marry someone who was born after WWII. If that makes me picky, I can accept that."

"So tell me about the bakery."

I plopped myself comfortably into the corner of the couch, picking up a pillow and hugging it as I looked out the front window at the cold, gray day. A short, stocky worker with a flattop was in the backyard. He pulled a two-by-four out from under a large blue tarp that protected the lumber supply from the Seattle drizzle.

"They're making progress," I said.

"How does it look? Take a bite, Izzy." Kate was multi-tasking. I wished I was, but instead I just sat and stared out the window.

"They spent several days tearing down walls and pulling up floors. They filled up one of those big dumpsters twice. I must have looked shocked when I saw how ripped up it was 'cause Dane told me not to panic."

"I can't wait to see it! I was thinking of driving over with Izzy later in the week."

"You should! You know, I'm going to need you to help me decorate the place. I want it to be really pretty and romantic and comfortable inside, and you're much better with interior decorating than I am."

"Ooh, you know I'd love to."

I watched Dane walk out the back door and over to the lumber. I knew I should move away from the window but, man, he made those faded jeans and long-sleeved, gray T-shirt look good. He threw back the tarp, picked up three large boards, and turned to walk back inside. As he swung around, our eyes met. He gave a little nod, the manly kind where the chin comes up, and looked like he was pleased to see me. I felt foolish that he'd caught me watching him but gave a little wave back.

"Abby, are you there?" Kate sounded exasperated.

"Yeah, I'm here."

"Where'd you go? I feel like I'm talking to myself."

"Oh, sorry. What'd you say?" I forced my attention back to Kate.

"I was asking you if you wanted to do a little shopping when I come this week. You know, start looking for ideas for the bakery."

"That'd be great. When do you want to go?" I was glad she hadn't asked why I was so distracted.

Saturday morning was bright and sunny. A lacy frost clung to the bushes and grass that were shaded by the house, but the rest of the world looked shiny and clear. As I looked out the front window, I noticed the tarp was only covering part of the lumber, so I slipped on some shoes and walked out the door to cover it up. As I tucked the tarp under one of the boards, I was surprised to hear the sound of hammering. We hadn't talked about the men working on Saturdays, and so far they'd taken weekends off.

I wanted to say thanks for the hard work so I headed for my little kitchen. Cheerful morning sunshine streamed through the window above the sink. I pulled out the ingredients for pumpkin muffins and set to work. Soon the smell of pumpkin and cinnamon filled the room. While the muffins baked, I changed my clothes, working hard to achieve that "I didn't work hard to look this good" look. I picked a white cable-knit sweater and my favorite pair of faded jeans. I tried pulling my hair up but then decided it looked better down.

By the time I took the muffins out of the oven, I was dressed and ready to express my appreciation for this extra effort with a tray of goodies and a thermos of hot cocoa with miniature marshmallows.

The back door to the bakery was slightly ajar, so I followed the sounds of hammering and a radio to the front room. Dane was on a ladder installing drywall. I looked around for the other guys, but Dane was working alone. I suddenly felt uncomfortable. Would he think I was being too forward?

"Hey, Abby. How ya doing?"

Why did I have to blush so easily?

"Hi, Dane. I didn't know you were going to work today. I thought I'd bring you a little snack." I moved over to a workbench and put down the tray.

"A *little* snack, huh?" Dane said, eyeing the three mugs, the tall thermos of hot cocoa, and half a dozen muffins.

"I thought the other guys were here too," I said. "I hope you're hungry."

"Actually, I'm starving. Those smell great." He laid down his hammer and climbed off the ladder.

"It's looking really good," I said as I started toward the door.

"Why don't you stay and have a muffin with me. I think there might be enough."

"I guess I could." This was turning out better than I'd planned, but

I still hoped he didn't think I'd planned it like this. I poured hot cocoa into the mugs as Dane took his first bite of muffin and sip of cocoa.

"Wow! This tastes even better than it smells. You didn't skimp on the marshmallows, did you?" he said.

"Hot cocoa just isn't the same without marshmallows."

"I think what you meant to say is that marshmallows aren't the same without a little hot cocoa," he said.

I laughed and felt my nervousness begin to slip away. "I thought they'd be completely melted by now."

Dane sat down on the floor, his back against the drywall. "Come sit down," he said, motioning with his muffin. I sat down a few feet away and sipped my cocoa. "These Seattle coffee drinkers don't know what they're missing," he said. He took a big swallow of hot cocoa and licked the marshmallow from his top lip.

"I know. Sometimes I feel like I must be one of the seven people in this city that don't drink coffee."

"I guess I'm another one of those seven. So, is it coming together the way you pictured it?"

"This big room is just what I wanted," I said. "I love the way the windows are looking." The two front windows had been expanded and now had larger than normal windowsills, ready for displaying wedding cakes that could be seen both inside the shop as well as from the street.

We talked about the crown molding, the original wood trim he'd stripped several coats of paint from, and the large, built-in shelves that could display more cakes. I lost track of time as we talked about the layout of the room, where the furniture would go, and decorating ideas.

"By the way," he said. "I found a beautiful antique door you might like at a little store in Snoqualmie. It's hand-carved and has a stained glass window. I don't think it would take much to size it to your opening here. I thought of you as soon as I saw it." I looked over at him, surprised. I was suddenly a little breathless. "I'm thinking you probably don't want to keep that ugly screen door."

"Oh, I don't know. The disco era has a unique charm."

"The disco era had a unique something," Dane said.

"How did you find a door in Snoqualmie?" I asked.

"I went skiing at Snoqualmie Pass last Saturday. I try to stop at this place in Snoqualmie whenever I can. They sometimes have windows or doorknobs that we use when we're restoring a house. I was hoping she'd have something that we could use here."

"Would I be stealing the door from one of your other projects?"

"If you don't want it, I might get it and hang onto it, but I can picture it right there. You should take a look at it. Maybe we can run out there sometime so you can see it."

"That'd be great." I tried not to appear overeager about the prospect of an outing together.

After nearly an hour and three muffins, Dane stood up and put his hand down to pull me up. He held my hand just a second longer than he had to, but not as long as I'd have liked him to. It made my own hand feel warm and tingly.

"Thanks. For the food and the company. That was just what I needed," he said.

"Good. I just wanted to say thanks for working on a Saturday." I gathered up the tray and mugs. I could feel his eyes on me as I left. I hoped he was smiling.

Five

Flaky Baking Powder Biscuits

2 cups sifted flour
1 Tbsp. sugar
4 tsp. baking powder
½ tsp. salt
½ cups shortening
1 egg, beaten
⅔ cups milk

Sift together flour, sugar, baking powder, and salt into bowl. Cut in shortening with pastry blender or two knives until mixture resembles coarse meal.

Combine egg and milk. Add to flour mixture all at once, stirring just enough with a fork to make a soft dough that sticks together (the secret to tender biscuits: don't overmix!).

Turn onto lightly floured surface and knead lightly 15 times. Roll to ¾-inch thickness. Cut with floured 2-inch cutter and place about 1-inch apart on an ungreased baking sheet.

Bake in 425°F oven for 12 minutes or until golden brown. Serve immediately.

*T*hings were moving along at a good pace. The bakery was taking on a new identity. I hardly remembered the way it had looked before we started the transformation. The walls of the showroom were painted a warm shade of ivory, while the kitchen walls were a clean, bright white. In just a few days, the floors would go in—a dark, wide-plank hardwood in the showroom that matched the woodwork around the door frames, and a retro black and white checked linoleum tile in the kitchen.

Time was flying. We were halfway to the April 28 opening. Every time I checked something off one of my lists, it seemed I thought of one or two more things to add. There was so much to do. Most of the time I enjoyed the excitement of this new chapter in my life, but every once in awhile, panic would grip my heart. At those moments, I'd give myself a pep talk and say a prayer. I felt Aunt Grace's confidence in me, and I forced myself to move systematically through the tasks on my lists.

"This is fantastic," Kate said as I showed her around one afternoon. "It doesn't even look like a house anymore." After a quick tour, we headed downtown to shop for furnishings.

Dane knocked on my door within a minute of my return home. "I was hoping that was you I heard drive in. I've been waiting for you all afternoon."

"You have?" I tried not sound too thrilled by his words.

"Your sign came. I wanted you to see it so we could get it put up before Elliot went home."

"Ooh, I can't wait to see it," I said. I grabbed the jacket I'd just taken off and we walked across the yard. In the front showroom of the bakery, the sign was on the floor on a large piece of cardboard. It was much bigger than I'd expected.

After we'd picked out a name for the bakery, I'd found a cute old man named Harvey Stewart. He looked about a hundred years old and had worked with iron most of that time. We sat down together and designed a sign to hang outside the front door. It had intricate wrought-iron details and a dropped wooden signboard that read "A Piece of Cake." Underneath the name were the words "Fine Wedding Cakes." It looked like a shingle from Victorian England, which I loved since the tradition of wedding cakes came from that time. "It's perfect," I said. "I got home too late to hang it today, didn't I?" I tried not to sound too disappointed.

"Elliot left almost an hour ago," Dane said.

"Why are you still here?"

"I've just been doing some little odds and ends. I was hoping you weren't going to be too late 'cause I wanted you to see it."

"Sorry I took so long. We found some great things, but it would have been nice to get this up today."

"You know, if you want to help me, I think we can get it up before I leave."

"Really?" I asked.

"We can give it a try."

Dane put the ladder beside the front door and screwed some brackets into the wall. Together, we carried the sign outside. It was heavy and bulky. I stood a few rungs below him and helped hold the sign as he guided it onto the brackets. My arms ached from the weight, but soon Dane had it bolted securely above and to the left of the front door. He climbed down and moved the ladder aside.

The sun had just set and it was harder to see. Dane reached inside the front door and flipped on a light switch. We stepped back to take a look. Two spotlights were anchored in the ground. He adjusted the direction so they lit each side of the sign.

"Did you do that?" I asked.

"Yeah," he said. "I thought it would be nice to see it at night too. It's the third switch just inside the door."

"Wow. Thank you."

"Sure." We stood looking at the sign in silence until it began to get uncomfortable. Suddenly Dane's stomach growled loudly. I pretended I hadn't heard it, but a moment later it rumbled again, and I burst out laughing.

Dane looked embarrassed. "I haven't eaten for at least seven hours. There's a little café around the corner on Chinook. Let's walk over and get something to eat."

I wasn't hungry at all. Kate and I had stopped for hamburgers just before she brought me home, but of course I was going to accept the offer, even if it meant eating a second dinner.

After enjoying bowls of corn chowder with bacon and flaky biscuits, we walked back. As we turned the corner onto my street, I stopped in my tracks. There was the sign. It looked elegant and professional. The lights illuminated the words, and the ornate iron curlicues made interesting shadows on the walls. We stopped in front of the bakery and stood there looking at it. I thought of how proud Aunt Grace would be, and a thrill of excitement made me shiver as we went inside.

I tried to stay out of the way when they were installing the floors. I worked at home and continued my shopping, crossing off a few more items on my lists. Late on the third evening, I looked out the front window and was surprised to see the lights still on in the bakery. They were working later than usual.

The floors were such a milestone. Once they were in, the appliances could be delivered—a huge Blodgett oven that could bake six layers at a time and two 72-cubic-foot commercial refrigerators. I couldn't wait to see all that stainless steel in my kitchen. I closed the blinds and went to the sink to wash up the evening dishes, imagining what my bakery kitchen would look like in just a few days. A knock at the door startled me out of my stainless steel daydream. I dried my hands and parted the blinds to see Dane on the porch. He smiled and waved.

"Hi," I said as I swung open the door. "You guys are working late."

"I wanted to stay until the floors were finished. You ready to see them?" There was an excitement in his voice that made me even more eager. I pulled the door shut behind me and a minute later, we were at the back door. We stepped inside to a black and white vision. Eighteen-inch black and white squares were set on the diagonal. The floor was swept clean and polished. Black rubber baseboards met the clean white walls.

"I love it!" I said.

"Okay, now close your eyes." I closed my eyes and Dane pushed open the swinging door to the showroom. He took my elbow to guide me through the door, and for a moment I lost interest in the floors. He led me a few steps into the room, then said, "Okay, open your eyes."

What a difference the floor made. The room looked finished. "This is fantastic!" I said. The room felt warm and inviting. It was easy to picture the room with cakes displayed and customers looking around. I was really opening a bakery, and it was actually mine. And it was so pretty.

It suddenly occurred to me that the wood was swept and polished.

"Do the installers always polish the floors?" I asked.

"Not usually," he said, looking around the room.

Something in his voice made me suspicious. "Did you polish them?" I asked.

"I didn't want them to be dusty and dirty the first time you saw them," he said.

I looked around the room and then at Dane. He was smiling at me—not the amused smile with the wrinkling around the eyes I'd seen so often, but a wide, happy smile. I wanted to walk straight over and give him a hug, but instead we just stood there smiling at each other until we both laughed.

"Thanks, Dane," I said when we'd reached my front porch. "It looks like a real bakery. I don't know if I've ever seen anything so beautiful!"

He looked at me, his face serious. "I have." He reached up and tucked a strand of hair behind my ear and then held it there for a second, his thumb brushing my cheek. I caught my breath. I didn't want him to move. "I'll see you tomorrow," he finally said as he reached around me and opened the front door. Then he turned and walked back toward the bakery.

He was halfway across the lawn when I finally found my voice. "Thanks, Dane," I said.

"You're welcome." At the door of the bakery, he turned around and waved. I stood there in the light from my open door. One by one the lights inside went off until the bakery was dark, and still I stood there hardly breathing. I listened intently as the front door of the bakery closed. Then I heard Dane close the door of his truck, start the ignition, and drive away. I didn't move.

I stood there until cold air had filled my little living room and I was nearly frozen through. Finally I went inside and locked the door. *What is happening here?* Whatever it was, I liked it.

Six

Fondant Daisies

fondant mat
fondant
small rolling pin
10-petal daisy cutter
thin foam mat
ball and veining tool

Knead fondant until it becomes soft. Shape it into a ball. Place in the center of the fondant mat. Use a rolling pin to flatten the fondant until it's as thin as possible.

Cut out two blossoms for each fondant flower—press firmly to get a clean cutout. Use a knife to gently remove excess fondant from the outer edges of the cutter. Place the pieces in a sealed container or under an inverted bowl.

Remove one fondant cutout from the container. Place it on your foam mat. Run the veining edge of the tool from the center of a petal to its edge. Repeat this process on each petal.

Remove another fondant cutout from the container. Repeat the veining process.

Dip your fingertip into water and dampen the top center of one of the pieces. Attach the other piece. Stagger the petals as you attach the blossoms.

The center of the flower can be made either with royal icing or by attaching a tiny ball of fondant.

ᴄᴏᴏ◈ᴄᴏ

*B*akery construction was winding down. Opening day was just a few weeks away, and although there was much to do, the bakery would be ready on time. Most days now, Dane worked alone, completing the shelves in the basement and the little office off the kitchen. His work would soon be finished.

The corner of the showroom was stacked with furnishings waiting to be unpacked—tablecloths, a thick oriental rug, and a few pieces of art. The furniture would arrive in four days—a robin-egg blue velvet couch, two cream and brown upholstered chairs, and an antique coffee table for a consultation area. A simple desk and two wooden armchairs would fill the corner. Three display tables would showcase cakes. Those along with the two front windows and the built-in shelves gave me room to display about ten dummy cakes.

Dummy cakes are both fun and disappointing to make. Styrofoam forms provide an ideal foundation. They're stronger and lighter than real cake—and much more forgiving—so dummy cakes can be architectural masterpieces. Each dummy cake I'd made over the past few weeks was intricate and exciting. But when I looked at them, I felt dissatisfied for some reason. They seemed a little phony. A real cake has life and heart and personality, while a dummy cake seems empty and hollow.

Still, the dummy cakes were turning out better than I'd hoped. And they were taking over my little house. I had them stacked on kitchen counters, stools, the coffee table, and even on my bedroom dresser. I was eager to display them properly in the showroom.

I was working on the last display cake when Dane showed up. "You busy?"

"I'm almost done. What's up?"

"You feel like a drive to Snoqualmie?"

"To see the door? Sure!" I quickly changed into khakis, a white turtleneck, and a denim jacket. When I came out, Dane was inspecting the display cake sitting on the coffee table. It was three tiers covered in fondant. Garlands of royal icing vines and leaves adorned the sides. Lifelike fondant daisies were placed at the top and bottom of each swag.

Dane looked up as I walked back in. "That really looks great. You've done this before, huh?"

"A few times. Some of these are similar to cakes I've seen in magazines, but this one is my own design."

"It looks hard," he said, and I tried not to feel too pleased.

A cold wind was blowing, but it was warm inside Dane's truck. It had been raining all day, and clouds darkened the sky. A wall of gray rain surrounded the truck, and it felt like we were separated from the rest of the world. I glanced at him as he drove and wished this was a real date instead of a drive to look at building supplies.

The main street in Snoqualmie runs parallel to abandoned railroad tracks. A couple of old railroad cars sit on the tracks on permanent display. As we passed them, a shaft of afternoon sun broke through the clouds and shimmered on the wet train cars. The windows and water reflected the light, and for a few moments the world was magical and golden. A block later, the clouds moved over the sun and everything returned to gray and green.

On the outskirts of town, we pulled into the gravel driveway of an old gingerbread house that looked like it had leapt off the pages of a colorful fairy tale. It was four shades of purple with a wide, wrap-around porch. Two weathered rocking chairs sat side by side, moving slowly in the gentle wind. The house was charming in spite of its garishness. An old, black buggy with "Annie's Antiques" painted on the side stood in the front yard. Dane knocked on the front door, and tiny, ancient Annie answered.

"There you are. I was afraid the rain might keep you away."

"I was born here. I've got webbed feet."

Annie chuckled. "And who is this pretty girl you brought with you?"

"This is my friend Abby. She's the one that's opening the bakery." Dane said.

"You didn't tell me she was such a beauty," Annie said, emphasizing her words by pointing her crooked finger at Dane.

"I guess I should have mentioned that." Dane smiled, and I felt the color rise in my cheeks.

"Well, kiddos, let's go on back to the shed."

We followed Annie's short, shuffling steps into the backyard. The "shed" was actually more like a barn—big enough to store mountains of odds and ends. Dane helped her swing open the big door. As my eyes adjusted to the dim lighting, I looked around me. The place was full of dusty collectibles. And then I saw the door, the reason for our trip.

I knew immediately why Dane had wanted me to see it. The door was solid and heavy and almost matched the wood floors in the showroom. In the top of the door was an oval stained-glass window with pink and red roses. The lower panel was adorned with hand-carved leaves. It had an antique bronze lever handle.

I reached out and ran my hand over the roses and felt the black, leaded lines outlining each leaf and petal. The wood had the time-polished feel of an antique. Its nicks and scratches added to its charm. I knew it belonged in the bakery. "It's perfect."

"I thought you'd like it," Dane said.

"You don't find a door like this very often," Annie added. "It's from a mansion in St. Louis, you know. When the family moved to Washington, the lady of the house said she wasn't moving without the door, so they shipped it out on the train and put it in the house they were building in Falls City. Then last year, some youngster bought the house and started remodeling. He called to see if I wanted it or if he should throw it away. Can you imagine throwing something like this away?" She clicked her tongue and shook her head.

"Thank goodness you got it," I said.

"Abby has just the right place for it," Dane said.

"I'm so glad. A treasure like this should be loved and admired, not left to gather dust in an old lady's shed."

I paid Annie, and Dane and I carefully wrapped the door in several blankets, laid it in the back of the truck, and covered it with a tarp as Annie watched.

"You kids enjoy that door." She gave a little wave and then bustled back to the shelter of the porch.

"Are you in a hurry to get back?" Dane asked.

"Not really." I was more than willing to extend the evening a little longer.

"Let's stop and take a look at the falls."

We drove down a few miles of winding road and parked in a deserted lot. The rain had stopped, but a cold, gusty wind blew. We walked past the closed gift shop to the observation deck. Snoqualmie

Falls is 270 feet of water crashing to the river below. Mist swirled from the waterfall and rose to meet us. The roar of the water reminded me of a scene from *Last of the Mohicans,* and I could imagine Hawkeye pledging to find Cora somewhere behind that violent water.

Dane stood close to me as we leaned over the wooden rail fence. I could feel my hair beginning to frizz in the spray, but I felt so exhilarated I didn't want to move.

A covered platform peeked from among the trees a hundred yards down a trail. "Let's check out the view from down there," Dane said and led the way down the path.

The roar of the water was farther away, but the air was still cold and damp. We sat together on a little bench and looked at the water. Evening was falling and lights twinkled in the windows of the lodge that overlooked the falls. It wasn't long before I began to shiver.

"You're freezing," Dane said. He moved closer and put his arm around my shoulders.

"A little bit."

"Do you want to go?"

Was he kidding?

I shook my head and leaned a little closer. And then Dane took my hand and held it. I don't know how long we sat like that. Stars began to twinkle in the velvet sky. I wanted time to stop and leave us there— close and happy.

"What made you decide to be a baker?" he asked me.

"I've always loved to bake. I started out with the usual things— cookies, bread, and pies."

"Mmm. Sounds good."

"Not always. I used to think chocolate chips made everything better. Then one time I made some tomato bread with chocolate chips, and I could tell that everyone who tasted it wanted to spit it out. I learned my lesson."

He laughed. "Are you all ready to open?"

"I think so. There are still a few things to get done, but I think I'm just about there."

"I finished the shelves in the basement today. I think you'll like how it's turned out."

"You've done a good job," I said. And then it hit me. The job was almost finished. Dane would move on to another job, I'd open the bakery, and then what? The excitement I'd felt all evening suddenly changed to uncertainty.

Dane seemed to sense what I was feeling. "It's going to be great, you know."

"I know."

"Hey, are you okay?" he asked, looking at me in the dim light. I nodded and tried to smile. Without a word, he wrapped his arms around me and pulled me closer. I hugged him back tightly, surprised at the intensity of my feelings. I barely breathed as he kissed the top of my head. "You're going to be fine," he said. "You're going to be more than fine. Don't worry."

"I'm trying not to," I said. "I love how the bakery's turned out. I'm a lucky girl."

"We're both lucky." His eyes held mine and my insides felt warm and melty. He touched my cheek softly, then lifted my face and gently kissed me on the lips. It was a perfect kiss that lingered a long, wonderful moment and left me with an ache that I knew would last until he kissed me again.

Later, I replayed the evening over and over in my mind before I finally fell asleep remembering the feel of Dane's arms around me and his lips on mine.

Seven

Homemade Egg Noodles

2 cups flour
3 egg yolks
1 egg
2 tsp. salt
¼–½ cup water

Measure flour into bowl; make a well in the center and add egg yolks, whole egg, and salt. With hands, thoroughly mix egg into flour.

Add water, 1 tablespoon at a time, mixing thoroughly after each addition. (Add only enough water to form dough into a ball.)

Turn dough onto well-floured board; knead until smooth and elastic, about 10 minutes. Cover and let rest for 10 minutes.

Roll dough into paper-thin rectangle. Cut desired thickness with a knife or kitchen scissors. Noodles can be dried for later use or added immediately to soup.

*T*he next week Kate dropped Izzy off to play at Grandma's and helped me set up the bakery. We assembled display tables and pressed the silk tablecloths that billowed like ivory clouds against the dark wood floor.

On the floor of the consultation area was a taupe Oriental rug covered with bluebirds and roses that matched those in the door. The robin-egg-blue couch added a splash of color to the otherwise soft and muted room. We hung drawings of brides from different eras on the wall. The earliest, from the 1800s, was holding a bouquet of daisies and wore a gown that sported a bustle. The latest, from the 1950s, wore a tea-length, full-skirted dress and a short veil attached to a pillbox hat.

We moved the display cakes to the bakery, and when the last cake was properly displayed, we fell onto the couch, exhausted.

"Wow, Abby," Kate said, looking around the room. "I don't think I've ever seen a prettier bakery. You must be so excited."

I sat up straight and turned to face her. "I'm scared to death. What if I have something this good and I mess it up?"

"You're not going to mess it up. Look at what you've done so far. Look at those." She pointed at the cakes across the room. "You were born to do this."

"I know how to make a cake, but I've never run a business before. I'm afraid I'll blow it."

Kate grabbed my hand. "Listen, Abby, you'll learn as you go. Of course, you'll make mistakes, but you'll figure it out. You're hardworking and smart. Aunt Grace knew that. We all know it. Have faith in yourself!"

I squeezed her hand tightly. Not only was she a good sister, she was also my best friend and my very own cheerleader. "You're right. I'll be fine." I was speaking more to myself than to Kate.

"Yes, you will."

⋯⊰✣⊱⋯

Our monthly family dinner was just six days before the grand opening. I was so exhausted I almost bowed out in favor of an afternoon of uninterrupted sleep, but then Kate reminded me that Mom was making chicken noodle soup with homemade noodles. As good as sleep sounded, the noodles sounded better.

"I'm excited to see the showroom now that you've got it all set up," Mom said.

"What do you have left to do?" Sam asked.

"I have to order pricing sheets and then do some baking the day before the open house."

"I think giving out samples is a good idea," Dad said. "It works for Costco."

"Oh, and I need something to deliver cakes in. Some kind of van, I guess."

"Is a minivan big enough?" Sam asked. "It would get better gas mileage than a full-sized one."

"That's what I was thinking," Dad said. "Mom and I could come car shopping with you if you want another opinion."

"That would be nice," I said.

"Do you still want us to help bake on Friday?" Mom asked.

"That's the plan," I said. I'd placed an advertisement in the Seattle Times Living section, but I had no idea how many people would show up.

"What are you charging for the cakes?" Evan asked.

I sighed heavily. "I don't know. I've got to come up with prices by Tuesday or I won't get everything back from the printer in time."

"Have you looked at what other bakeries charge?" asked Kate.

"Yes, and the prices are all over the place."

"I'd say it depends," Evan said. "Do you want to make your cakes for average people or do you want to cater to a high-end market?"

"That's just it. I don't even know. Can I even hope to get the high-end business? I'm just starting out."

"Lower prices might bring in more business," said Sam.

"Well, for what it's worth," Mom said, "I think you could charge whatever you want! Your cakes are fantastic." Spoken like a true mom.

"But what do you think people will actually pay? I know my cakes are good, but don't I have to pay my dues first?"

"Well, a product is worth whatever people are willing to pay," said Dad. "The problem is you don't know what that is yet."

At that moment an idea leaped into my mind. It wasn't a spark, and it didn't evolve. It landed there as a fully formed idea. I didn't even have a chance to think about how crazy I might sound before it spilled out of my mouth. "Well, if a product is worth what people are willing to pay, why not let the people decide how much they should pay?"

Everyone laughed. They thought I was joking. Only I wasn't laughing.

"I'm serious." I said. "What if I let people decide what their wedding cake is worth and that's what they pay?"

"Yeah, right, Abby. That idea isn't riddled with problems," Evan said, rolling his eyes.

"What are the problems?" I needed to talk through this. Was I crazy? "Wait! Keep thinking." I ran to the kitchen and got a notebook and pen. I moved my bowl aside and laid out the notebook, ignoring the incredulous looks around the table. At the top of the left page, I wrote "Pros" and at the top of the right page, I wrote "Cons."

"Ooh, we get to help with one of Abby's lists," Evan said. He was teasing me, but he leaned forward in his chair, ready to offer his two cents. Now we were rolling. The idea excited me, but I could tell almost everyone else thought I'd lost my mind.

"Big con," Dad said. "People will take advantage of you."

"Some will," said Kate, "but not all. Some people might actually pay more so they won't look cheap."

"What if some people think they aren't worth anything?" asked Evan.

"Then they won't pay anything," I said.

"That won't help your bottom line," said Dad. By now no one was eating. They kept looking at each other, wondering how to bring me to my senses.

"Do you really think anyone would pay nothing for a beautiful cake?" I asked.

"Yeah," said Dad. "There might be a few like that."

"That doesn't seem very likely," Mom said. "I can't imagine getting a cake and thinking I should pay nothing."

"If Abby gives people beautiful cakes and good experiences," said Kate, "they might be so caught up in the emotions that they'll decide to pay more than Abby would have charged in the first place."

While they talked I wrote. The more I wrote, the more I knew what I wanted to do.

When the discussion wound down, I laid down my pen and looked at my family. "I'm going to do it," I said. They looked at each other uneasily. "What have I got to lose? Think about it. Maybe it will flop. But what if it works? Aunt Grace left me enough to support the business for a year. I'll do this for a few months and if it works, great! If it doesn't, then I can set my prices. But at least then I'll have some experience, and maybe I'll have a better idea what I should charge."

Mom and Kate were the first to smile and give a little nod. Eventually, Dad joined in. "You know," he said, "if nothing else, this will be quite an interesting little experiment."

Eight

Ivar's Clam Chowder

1 cup finely chopped onions
1 cup finely diced celery
2 cups finely diced potatoes
¾ cup butter
2 (6½-oz.) cans minced clams
¾ cup flour
4 cups half-and-half, warmed
1 tsp. salt (to taste)
dash pepper
½ tsp. sugar

Combine onions, celery, and potatoes in a pan. Add enough water to barely cover. Simmer, covered, over medium heat until the potatoes are tender, about 20 minutes.

In a medium saucepan, melt the butter. Add the juice from the clams; set the clams aside. Whisk in the flour until smooth. Add the half-and-half. Cook and whisk until smooth and thick, about 5 minutes. If you want thinner chowder, add ½ to ¾ cup water or clam broth.

Add the vegetables with their cooking liquid, clams, salt, pepper, and sugar to the pan.

Stir well and adjust the seasonings if necessary.

*W*ith my pricing dilemma resolved, I finished my brochure and took it to the printer. Under "Deposit," it said $50.00. Under the "Price of Cake" heading, it said "You Decide." The Kenny Rogers look-alike behind the counter examined it and then eyed me quizzically. "Are you sure about this?" he asked.

"I'm sure," I said.

"They'll be ready on Thursday." He turned away from the counter, shaking his head.

"Thanks," I said to his back.

It was a funny thing. I'd worried for weeks about everything I was doing. Was the shop elegant enough? Had I chosen the best cakes to display? Did I have the right appliances? But for some reason, when it came to my pricing scheme, I hadn't questioned myself. I couldn't wait to see what would happen.

❦

That night I ate dinner in front of the television. It had been weeks since I'd watched an entire TV show, and it felt good to put my feet up and relax to The Food Network. At about eight, Dane called.

"Hi, Abby. How's it going?"

"I'm good. Tired, but good."

"I drove by on Sunday, but you weren't home."

"You did?" I felt simultaneously thrilled and disappointed.

"I just thought maybe we could go for a drive." This call was getting better by the second.

"I went out to Bellevue and had dinner with my family. Sorry I missed you."

"No problem. I saw the cakes in the window. It looks like you're about ready to go."

"It's getting close. I took the brochures to the printer today and Mom and Kate are coming to bake with me on Friday."

"Well, I don't think you want me in the kitchen, but is there anything else you need help with?"

"You know, you might surprise yourself and be a natural at whipping up icing. It could be one of your hidden talents."

"I doubt it. But you can call me if you get desperate. Is there something I can do for you that doesn't require an apron?"

"Well, I have to buy a car."

"Now that's more like it."

"Well, actually a minivan. I need something reliable to deliver cakes with and everyone thinks a minivan is the way to go."

"Minivan shopping, huh? I've never done that on a date before. But sure, I can help you with that." He'd said date. We were going on a real date.

"I was planning to go sometime in the next couple of days."

"How about tomorrow?" he asked.

"Sure."

"I'll pick you up at four?"

"Sounds good."

"And don't eat dinner."

"Okay."

"Okay."

"Okay," I said again, frustrated that witty banter refused to come to me. Why was it that Jane Austen's heroines could always come up with clever quips and I sounded like a tongue-tied teenager? It was embarrassing.

He laughed. "I'll see you tomorrow then."

I hung up the phone and thought about Dane while I watched Rachael whip up a delicious meal of barbecued pork sandwiches with baked potato wedges and mini-cheesecakes in only thirty minutes. Then I called Dad and Mom and told them they wouldn't have to go car shopping after all. They weren't in the least put out that I was dumping them for a handsome, single, LDS man with steady employment.

As it turned out, minivan shopping could be a surprisingly romantic activity. When we got out of the truck at the first car lot, Dane casually held my hand. He seemed totally comfortable. Meanwhile, I felt like my entire consciousness had suddenly taken up residence in my hand.

Dane didn't say much, except to ask a few pointed questions that let the salesmen know they weren't dealing with chumps. We visited three car dealerships, test-drove four vans, and soon I was the proud owner of a white Honda Odyssey whose seats could be easily removed by a girl. Namely me.

"Congratulations," Dane said. "Now let's go celebrate. I'm starving."

Ivar's, which sat on the waterfront next to the port where the ferries came and went, had the best seafood anywhere in the Pacific Northwest. The main restaurant was expensive and hoity-toity, but there was also an open-air seafood bar for the more casual diner. The last time I'd eaten there was when Kate was pregnant with Izzy. The entire meal had been spent battling several fat and aggressive seagulls.

We ordered steaming clam chowder in bread bowls and sat under a large tent at a picnic table. Lights sparkled from a few boats out on the water. We watched the last ferry of the night leave for Bainbridge Island, and I told Dane about my pricing plan.

"Wow, that's courageous," he said.

"Do you think I'm crazy?" I really hoped he didn't.

"Maybe a little. But in a good way. A brave way. It'll be interesting to see how it turns out." He suddenly seemed thoughtful.

"What?" I asked.

"I was just wondering what you'd have paid me if we'd left it up to you," he said.

"What your work was worth? I'm not a millionaire, you know."

We stayed and talked until a busboy came to the tent to wipe off the tables and empty the trash cans. Then we walked across Alaskan Way to his parked truck and my minivan with the paper license plate in the back window. I was glad I wasn't alone. The parking lot under the noisy freeway was creepy after dark.

"Thanks for your help," I said. "It was nice having someone else there. You probably kept me from getting taken to the cleaners."

"I don't know about that. But I was glad to tag along." The freeway rattled as cars passed above us. "So Saturday's the big day."

"I'm trying not to think of it as doomsday."

"It's been a busy few months."

"And we made it in time for Aunt Grace's birthday, thanks to you."

"We did okay," he said. "If you need any help with anything else, just give me a call."

"I will."

"Do you mind if I stop by Saturday for a piece of cake?"

"Of course not. I'll be open from ten to eight."

"That's a long day."

"I just hope somebody shows up."

"Keep some sticks handy in case the mobs get out of hand."

"I'm glad you're so optimistic."

"They'd be crazy not to come." He leaned in and gave me a kiss on the cheek. He waved as he watched me drive away. It was several miles before the feeling of the kiss began to fade.

Nine

Candied Walnut Cream Cheese Filling

1½ cups walnuts
½ cup sugar
2 Tbsp. water
⅛ tsp. salt
8 oz. butter
8 oz. cream cheese, softened
4 cups powdered sugar
2 tsp. vanilla extract

Preheat oven to 350°F. Lay walnuts out on a baking sheet in a single layer. Toast for 5–7 minutes on middle rack of oven. Be careful not to burn. Remove from oven and let cool in pan on a rack.

Pour sugar and water into a medium saucepan with a thick bottom. Have walnuts nearby, ready to quickly add to the pan at the right time. Cook sugar on medium heat, stirring with a wooden spoon as soon as the sugar begins to melt. Keep stirring until all the sugar has melted and the color is a medium amber. Add the walnuts, stirring quickly to coat each piece with the sugar mixture.

As soon as the walnuts are coated with the sugar mixture, spread them out on a rimmed baking sheet, sprayed with Pam. Use two forks to separate the walnuts from each other, working quickly. Sprinkle the nuts with the salt. Let cool completely. Chop to desired size.

In a large bowl, beat together the butter and cream cheese with an electric mixer. With the mixer on low speed, add the powdered sugar a cup at a time until smooth and creamy. Beat in the vanilla extract. Mix in chopped candied walnuts.

I woke up before the alarm went off. The day of my open house had finally arrived. I felt a little frazzled as I scrambled two eggs and made toast. Although I knew it wasn't rational, it seemed like the success or failure of the bakery hinged on the next several hours.

My outlook was better after I'd eaten and showered, but the real attitude adjustment came when I pulled out the clothes Kate had insisted I buy. "You'll *feel* professional if you *look* professional," she'd said. She was right. The dress had an empire waist and a soft, flowing skirt. A cardigan with three-quarter length sleeves and a pair of low-heeled shoes finished the outfit. I pulled my hair up in a twist and even applied a rare touch of lipstick. *Do I look like the owner of a wedding cake shop?* I turned in front of the mirror and decided I did.

The sun was shining brighter than it had in weeks. There wasn't a single cloud in the sky, and as I walked across the lawn to the bakery, the air felt fresh and charged. Buds were forming on the rosebushes, green blades of grass were pushing up through the winter-brown lawn, and the world felt full of promise.

Evan arrived at 9:30, looking smart in gray slacks and a navy sweater. He brought four bouquets of tulips from Pike Place Market. I'd planned out the whole day carefully—Evan would stay and help me for a few hours. Mom would take the middle shift, and Kate would finish out the day. I was glad I didn't have to face the day alone.

Once the flowers were placed around the room, it looked like the bakery where Annie picks out her cake in *Father of the Bride*. We filled two silver platters and a porcelain pedestal cake stand with samples of chocolate ganache-filled raspberry mousse cake, chocolate butter cake with citrus buttercream, and carrot cake with candied walnut cream cheese filling. Evan ate a third sample and caught my look of disapproval. "I'll try to save some for the customers."

"Where did you find this?" Evan asked. He was looking at a Wayne Thiebaud print of about a dozen cakes on pedestals. I'd hung it on the wall behind the desk.

"I got that when Aunt Grace and I went to Washington, DC. We saw the original in the National Gallery."

"That was a long time ago. You've had it all this time?"

"Ten years. I got it framed for the bakery. I think of Aunt Grace whenever I look at it. I thought it was a good way to be sure she's always part of the bakery."

"She'd like that." He surveyed the room. "If I needed a wedding cake, I'd definitely come here."

"I certainly hope so," I said.

"You need to document this day. Where's your camera?" Evan retrieved the camera from my house, and we spent the next several minutes snapping pictures.

As of 10:30, no one had come. Evan tried to occupy me with a few horse stories, and we talked about our new wards. I allowed myself to be distracted for a while, but then I glanced at my watch.

"Abby, it's okay. People will come. Don't worry."

I looked at all the hard work growing stale around us and felt a little sick. I escaped to the kitchen for a glass of water. I stood at the sink and drank it slowly, trying to quiet the rising panic.

At 11:20, the phone rang. "A Piece of Cake, can I help you?"

"Is today your open house?" a woman asked.

"It is. We'll be here until eight this evening."

"What's the best way to get there?"

I gave the caller directions.

"See," Evan said after I'd hung up. I noticed the relief in his voice and knew he was worried too. "Someone's on their way."

I gave him a half-hearted thumbs up and sat down to await my potential customer. Noon arrived and still no one. I saw myself calling my old boss and telling him how much I missed the industrial sounds and smells of Harward and begging him for my job back.

The samples were looking as sad as a closing time all-you-can-eat buffet, so we dumped them in the garbage and filled the trays with fresh samples.

I suddenly hoped Dane wouldn't come. If he showed up and felt sorry for me, it would only make things worse.

At 12:30, the little bell above the door rang, announcing my first visitors—a young lady and an older woman, both with red hair.

"Hello. I'm Abby."

"I'm Jillian and this is my mom."

"I'm glad you could come. Just take a look around, try a few samples, and then I'll be glad to answer any questions you might have." Jillian and her mother began in the display cakes. The sound track to "The Man from Snowy River" drowned out their quiet conversation. They tried a couple of pieces of cake, and soon they were ready to talk to me.

"Could we see a price list?" the mother asked.

"Well . . ." Here it was. The speech I'd been practicing. I handed the mother a brochure. "The pricing is a little different than you've probably seen other places. I charge a fifty-dollar deposit to reserve your wedding date, and then the cake price will be what you decide it's worth."

"I'm afraid I don't understand," the mother said.

"I'll deliver the cake and an invoice, and then within a week after the wedding, you'll pay me what you think it was worth." Whew! I'd said it and they weren't running for the door.

Yet.

"Are you serious?" the bride asked.

"Absolutely." I smiled.

The bride's mother frowned. "You won't make any money that way!"

"Well, the cake will be delicious and beautiful," I said.

"I've never heard of such a thing." The mother was shaking her head. "I don't know, Jillie. Maybe this isn't for us." The mother gave her daughter a meaningful look and inclined her head toward the door.

"Please don't let the idea scare you. I can assure you that you'll get a quality cake and what you pay is up to you." I hoped I was sounding confident and not desperate. *Please don't walk out the door. Please.*

"What a great idea," Jillian said, and she picked up a design book off the coffee table. "So what's our next step?" She motioned to her mother, who reluctantly joined her daughter. I sat down and soon we were discussing ideas and details. Half an hour later, I had a fifty-dollar deposit, and my first wedding cake was booked for June 9.

"Good job, Abby," Evan said after the door closed. "I wasn't sure you could pull it off. That mother was scared to death."

"I know. When I saw her face, I thought maybe I'd made a big mistake. But she booked!" I did a little celebration dance, and we gave each other a high five. "Now if we can just get more people to check us out," I said.

"They'll come."

"Evan, you could double my business if you'd just find a nice girl to marry."

"Maybe I'll surprise you someday," he said. I saw something in his expression that made me curious, but before I could ask about it, Mom walked in.

"Hey, kids, have you been busy?"

Evan and I laughed. "No, but I did get one booking."

"Well, I'm sure it will pick up," Mom said.

Evan hugged me good-bye. "Don't get discouraged," he said. He grabbed another piece of cake, kissed Mom on the cheek, and left.

Mom sat down, and we tried to chat, but it was hard to carry on a conversation when all I could think about was that no one was coming. Now time really dragged. It was much harder having no customers with Mom here than it had been with Evan. Evan had tried to distract me. But the way Mom fretted and tried to figure out ways to solve the problem, I felt like I needed to distract *her*. After a while, Mom went back to my house. A few minutes later, she reappeared with two peanut butter and jelly sandwiches, which we ate at the desk.

We replaced the dried-out samples for the second time. It made me sad to waste them after all our hard work. We walked around the display cakes, while Mom had me describe how I'd made each one. The minute hand on my watch crawled. Mom looked deflated. "You'll be in the phone book that comes out the end of June, right?"

"Yes, I have a two-inch advertisement with my listing."

"That should bring in some good business."

"And I'm going to a bridal show this fall at the trade center."

"Good. I'm sure that will help."

Just after 2:30, a young couple came through the door. Before I was through helping them, a bride-to-be arrived with two of her friends.

And then the storm broke. People began to pour into the shop.

They looked through books, they tasted the samples, and they wanted to talk to me all at once. Several times, customers were waiting in line to talk to me. It was so busy, I hardly noticed when Kate arrived and Mom left. Kate replenished the samples and talked to the waiting mob. I hardly had time to breathe. Although everyone was surprised by the method of pricing, no one left because of it. Maybe the more timorous were reassured that so many other people were booking cakes.

By the time I closed the door behind the last customer, my feet were on fire and I was bone tired.

Kate and I sat down at the desk and transferred all of the day's bookings to a calendar. I could hardly wait to see how many there were. "Wow, Abby! Fourteen! This is a great start!" I was thrilled.

"That's more than I thought."

"Look at this. You have a wedding cake scheduled for May 9. That's less than two weeks away."

"And I think the last one is in October. Is that right?" I asked.

She thumbed through the calendar. "October 14. You outdid yourself, huh?"

"I'd have been happy with six or eight. I'd say this is a pretty good start."

"And you'll get more business once you start delivering these beautiful cakes. They say word of mouth is the best advertising." Kate stretched and yawned. "You must be shot. I'm tired, and I was only here for the last four hours."

"I'm pretty wiped out. And hungry!"

"Oh! I forgot to tell you. That guy, Dane, called while you were busy with a customer."

"What did he say?" I tried to sound casual.

"When I told him how busy it was, he said he'd wait and stop by after you closed. He said he'd bring Chinese food about 8:30." As if on cue, I heard his truck pull into the driveway. Kate stood up. "I'd better get going."

"Stay and eat with us. You've got to be hungry too."

"I don't know. I really should be getting home," Kate said.

"Oh brother. Just stay for a little while, then you can go. Besides, don't you want to meet Dane?"

Kate eyed me suspiciously.

"Is there any particular reason I should be meeting him?" she asked.

"I don't know. Why don't you stick around for a while and see."

"I'll stay and eat if he brought enough food. But don't make a big deal about it."

I opened the door to meet Dane. It was obvious by the size of the bag he carried that there was plenty of food. We sat around the desk, eating with chopsticks and talking about the day. Now that it was over, we could laugh at the morning's slow start. They enjoyed my account of the first mother's reaction to the "you decide" pricing.

Before long, Kate stood to leave. I hugged her good-bye at the door.

"Thanks for all your help, Kate. You've been a lifesaver. I don't know what I would've done without you and Mom and Evan today."

"It was fun. This is pretty cool, Abby. All of it," she said and directed a meaningful glance toward the desk where Dane was cleaning up the remains of our meal. "I think you've got some explaining to do."

"I don't know what you're talking about," I said.

I closed the door behind her and leaned against it. I felt lighter and freer than I had in weeks.

"Do you have to run?" I asked Dane.

"No, what do you have in mind?"

"Let's watch a movie. I haven't seen one for more than three months."

"Sounds good. Why don't you go get changed, and I'll finish cleaning up."

"Be sure to grab a few of the samples," I said from the back door.

"Dkwu kyu wkarr," he said. I had no idea what he said because his mouth was already full of cake.

Fifteen minutes later, I was in comfortable flannel pants and a sweatshirt and we were watching *Leap Year*. Dane put his arm around me and I tucked my legs up comfortably. I didn't wake up until I heard Dane turn off the TV.

"Aren't we going to finish the show?" I asked.

Dane laughed. "We did. It's over."

"You're joking," I said. "Why didn't you wake me up?"

"You looked way too comfortable, and I think you needed the rest."

"Please tell me I didn't snore."

"You didn't snore. It was the talking in your sleep that was the most entertaining," he said.

"Oh, no! You should've poked me or something."

He put out his hand and pulled me up beside him. "You need to get to bed."

"I'm sorry I was such terrible company tonight."

"You won't hear any complaints from me. You get a good night's sleep, and I'll call you tomorrow." He walked to the door.

"I'm glad you came over tonight," I said.

"I'm glad your open house was a hit."

"Me too," I said, and I put my arms around him. "And thanks for bringing dinner."

"You're welcome." He leaned down and kissed me on the forehead.

"And thanks for finding that beautiful door."

"You're welcome," he said and kissed me on the nose.

I liked where this was headed. "And thanks for doing such a good job on the shop."

This time, he didn't say anything. He just kissed me, long and slow. If he hadn't had his arms around me, I might have toppled over. He pulled back and looked down at me for a long time like he wanted to say something. But he didn't. Instead, he kissed me once more and then opened the door and left.

Ten

Toasted Almond Ganache Filling

"Ganache" is a French term referring to a smooth mixture of chopped chocolate and heavy cream. It was probably invented around 1850. Some say it originated in Switzerland, where it was used as a base for truffles. Others say it was invented in Paris at the Patisserie Siravdin.

¾ cup slivered almonds, toasted
1 cup heavy whipping cream
2 cups semisweet chocolate chips

Preheat oven to 350°F. Place almonds in a single layer on a baking sheet. Toast in oven for 5–7 minutes. Cool and chop.

In a saucepan, heat cream to just before boiling. Remove from heat. Pour in the chocolate chips and cover pan. Let the pan rest for 10 minutes. Gently stir the melted chocolate and cream together. Add chopped almonds, stirring gently to avoid air bubbles. Let cool for an hour.

*W*ithin a couple of weeks, I'd fallen into a comfortable work routine. I spent mornings working in the shop. In the afternoon, I'd forward my bakery calls to my cell phone and work at home or run errands. Since I hadn't made a wedding cake for a client, it almost felt like I was a little girl playing bakery. I tried to enjoy the relaxed pace, but I was so excited to start delivering real wedding cakes to real weddings that I began to grow impatient.

Dane and I went to a movie on Friday evening. The movie was just so-so, but sitting together and holding hands more than made up for it. Afterward we went to a little all-night diner and ordered pecan waffles and hot cocoa.

I'd expected to feel anxious on the day of my first cake, but instead I felt calm and relaxed. The bride had chosen a different flavor for each of the three tiers. I was unhurried and precise as I baked and assembled the cake. After the layers had cooled, I circled the top of each cake with a wide band of buttercream icing. I filled the layers of the lemon cream tier with a Bavarian cream pudding and fresh raspberries and topped it with another layer. A quick crumb coat and the first tier was in the cooler.

The scent of toasted almonds filled the kitchen. I pulled them out of the oven, chopped them, and added them to the ganache. This was my favorite filling, and I treated myself to a spoonful before I filled the chocolate tier of cake. The top tier was a carrot cake with a simple cream cheese filling.

I measured and cut dowels to insert for support in the two lower layers and then re-frosted each tier with a sweet, pale buttercream icing.

Now came my favorite part.

I pried the lid off my first twenty-five pound tub of fondant. Up to this point in my life, I'd always bought five pound boxes of fondant. Opening a twenty-five pound tub made me a little giddy.

I kneaded the fondant until it was soft and pliable. Then, using a two-foot rolling pin, I rolled it into a circle big enough to cover the bottom layer. I lifted the disc of flattened fondant and carefully worked it onto the cake, smoothing out any air pockets or creases. This was the tricky part. I'd seen too many fondant cakes with creases hidden behind flowers or decorations because the cake maker had been lazy or unskilled. Using a large pizza cutter, I cut off the excess fondant. I repeated the process for each of the other layers.

Once the layers were stacked, I rolled three pieces of fondant into long cords and braided them. These were the borders for each tier.

I stepped back to examine my work. It was just after noon, and I had a finished cake. It had the smooth luster of Lladró porcelain. The kitchen was warm and smelled sweet and nutty. I felt good.

That afternoon, I put a one-inch foam pad in the seatless back of the minivan, placed the cake on the pad, and headed out to make my first delivery. This was one part of owning a wedding cake shop that scared me. Driving a finished cake through the crowded streets of Seattle was about as relaxing as swimming in a tank of sharks. I had to drive at a speed that protected the cake without getting me rear-ended.

I reached the Old Hollywood Schoolhouse with my cargo intact. Inside the charming brick building, I found the cake table set in front of an exposed brick wall. I placed the cake on the pale yellow table-cloth and white eyelet topper and arranged some pink and yellow tulips around the base and on the top tier. I stepped back to inspect my work. I was pleased to see how well the background of rough, irregular bricks accentuated the dreamy whiteness of the cake. The contrast made me think of *Beauty and the Beast.*

I took a picture, trying not to look like I'd won the lottery, and wished I'd invited Mom or Kate to come and share this moment with me.

I took a deep breath, found Mrs. Atherton, the bride's mother, and handed her my invoice. I suddenly felt the absolute vulnerability of my situation. I'd gambled a lot of money and effort on this, and now I was completely at someone else's mercy. For the first time since I'd come up with my pricing scheme, I was scared. I no longer had any control over the matter. All I could do was cross my fingers and hope.

I dialed Mom's number as soon as I walked out the front door of the reception center. "Hi, Mom."

"Hi, Abby, how did it go?"

"Oh, Mom, I wish you could have seen it. What a great place for a wedding. It was this quaint, old brick schoolhouse, and the cake looked fantastic."

"Did anyone say anything about it?"

"Mrs. Atherton seemed very pleased. We'll see what happens next. I wish I'd have brought you with me. Will you come with me sometime?"

"I'd love to, honey."

Five days later, Mrs. Atherton walked into the shop and handed me a monogrammed envelope. "Abby, the cake was a hit. Celeste is in Hawaii, but she wanted me to tell you she loved it. I really didn't know what to pay, so I hope this is okay," she said.

"Thank you, Mrs. Atherton," I said. Through a superhuman effort I waited calmly while Mrs. Atherton got in her car and disappeared down the street. Then I ripped open the envelope. Inside was a card and a check, folded in half. I've always had a personal rule that I can't open a present until after I've read the card, so I resisted the urge to look at the check.

> *Dear Abby,*
> *Thank you for the beautiful wedding cake. It was just what I wanted, and I can't even tell you how many people commented on how delicious it was. It was a lovely finish to a lovely day. We'll be sure to refer all our friends to you. Thank you again.*
> *Celeste and Derek Jenkins*

Finally, I unfolded the check. It was written out for four hundred dollars.

For a week I'd gone back and forth between excitement and fear about this moment. Now I felt justified, even triumphant. But mostly I felt incredibly relieved.

⁓∞⊱✦⊰∞⁓

I was excited to share my good news at the family's monthly Sunday dinner.

"She gave Abby four hundred dollars." Kate was so excited that she blurted out the news before I could say a word.

Dad whistled. "Four hundred dollars. Were you happy with that?"

"I thought it was great. I only would have charged about three hundred."

"When's your next cake?" asked Mom.

"Thursday. It's a big one—five tiers with about eighty marzipan roses. I've been working on the roses for days now. Oh, and I got another order this week for a cake in June. That's six cakes set for June."

"Not bad after our slow morning," Evan said.

"Tell the truth, Evan. You were worried, weren't you?"

"A little," Evan said. "I didn't want you to be disappointed."

"What are you going to do when you get too busy to do it all yourself?" Sam asked.

"It'll probably be a long time before I have to worry about that, if ever."

"So, Abby, Kate tells us there's a young man we should know more about," Dad said.

"Well, Sam's nice, but I thought you already knew him," I said.

"You know we're not talking about Sam," Kate said.

"You already know about him, Dad. He's the contractor that remodeled the bakery. The one who helped me find the van."

"Yes, we know that," Mom said, "but if you're actually dating him, we need to know a little more about him than his ability to pick out doors and shop for cars, don't you think?"

"What do you want to know?"

"Everything," Dad said.

"Well, he works with his father. He did a really good job on the bakery." I wasn't sure what else to say. I didn't want to tell the entire family that I loved the crinkles around his eyes. I couldn't explain how my stomach did dances when he smiled at me. And I certainly didn't want to tell them that his kisses had knocked my knees out from under me.

"Tell them how handsome he is," said Kate.

"He's pretty good-looking, I guess," I said.

"And I think he really likes our Abby too," said Kate. I gave her a hard look that told her she'd said enough.

"Is he a good man?" Dad asked. I knew what Dad meant by "good." Dad didn't really care about his looks or about all the trivial details of his life. He was asking about Dane's character.

"Yes, Dad, he's a good man."

Dad nodded. "That's all that matters."

I didn't completely agree that that was *all* that mattered. I could think of a few other things that mattered to me. But it was nice to be dating a guy who didn't check out our waitresses or play juvenile mind games.

"We've only been on a couple of dates," I said.

"Maybe officially," said Kate, "but you've seen so much of him it's like you've been dating for months." She had a point.

"When do we get to meet him?" Mom asked.

"Maybe you could bring him to dinner," Evan said.

"Be careful," Sam said. "You don't want to scare him off."

"We didn't scare you off," I said.

"No, but it was close. It's a good thing Kate was so beautiful."

"*Was* so beautiful?" Kate asked.

"You know you *are* so beautiful."

Evan grimaced. "Either cut that out or get me a bucket."

"Do you think he could handle dinner with all of us?" Sam asked.

"I think he'd do okay. But you have to promise to be nice."

"We'll be nice," Dad said.

⌒◦◦❧◦◦⌒

It turned out I had nine cakes in June. I carefully attended to every detail of each cake. I didn't want to make any mistakes. I felt creative and artistic and couldn't imagine going back to answering questions about backhoes.

My favorite cake that month was a white-on-white polka dot cake. With royal icing, I piped circles in different sizes and then filled the circles with thinned royal icing. Once they dried, they looked like little porcelain domes. Once I attached them randomly on the cake, it began to look like something a glamorous Minnie Mouse would choose. When I saw the bride's short, baby-doll wedding dress, I knew I'd delivered the perfect cake.

Within a week of each delivery, I received payment. For the most part, I'd been pleased with the results. I thought some cakes were worth a little more than I'd been paid, but other customers paid more than I would have charged. It was averaging out pretty fairly. I was working hard to deliver high-quality wedding cakes, and it was paying off. I also found that every payment was like Christmas morning.

During this period, I found myself spending a lot of time thinking about what my cakes were really worth. Maybe that's why I started pondering the worth of other things in my life. I carefully weighed every purchase I made, and I soon realized that some of the things I'd been spending money on weren't really worth much at all.

After a while, I extended my evaluations to other things. I found myself turning off TV shows that didn't seem worth the investment of time and attention and reading good books instead.

Little did I know how soon I would be forced to weigh the value of far more important things.

Eleven

Sugar Baubles

3 cups sugar
1 cup water
1⅓ cups corn syrup
½ tsp. cream of tartar

Bring sugar, water, and corn syrup to a boil. Add cream of tartar and continue boiling until it reaches 314°F. Pour onto a marble slab or a large Silpat sheet. When cool enough to handle, pull off balls, marble to golf-ball size, depending on the size of bauble you want. Attach to the end of a wooden straw and blow. Twist the bauble and melt the end shut with a spirit burner and cut away with scissors. Caution: Be very careful. It is easy to burn yourself when working with hot sugar.

The thrill of new love and the excitement of marriage conspired to put most of my customers in a pretty good mood. Most of the brides arrived with a support system—a friend, a sister, a mother, or sometimes even a bewildered fiancé in tow. Then, on a cloudy day near the end of June, a new element presented itself—a mother-in-law.

The trio sitting across from me was a perfect match for the gloomy weather outside. The bride, who was young and petite with blonde hair, stared at the floor when I shook her hand. The groom's hair hung low over one eye, and he unsuccessfully flipped it off his face so often I thought he might give himself whiplash. He wore a yellow-and-white seersucker blazer and a plaid bow tie. He looked like he'd have preferred an invasive medical procedure to sitting through this consultation. He sat slouching between the women with his arms tightly crossed. His mother sat erect on the edge of her seat, gripping her Louis Vuitton purse in her crimson-nailed hands. Her back was ramrod straight, and she held her head so high that she actually had to look down her sharp nose at me.

It was immediately clear which of the three was in charge.

I opened my order book to a blank form. "Shall we get started?" I said.

"First things first," the mother-in-law said. "We need to know if you can handle a large cake on the 26th of July."

I'd checked my calendar. "That shouldn't be a problem."

"I'd really prefer that you not take any other cakes that day. I don't want you to have any distractions."

"I'll reserve that day just for you."

"And what about the day before? July 25. Are you free that day as well? I want you to have plenty of time to do our cake right."

I tried not to react, but her tone annoyed me. I was already wishing I'd told her I wasn't available, but the bakery was new, and I didn't feel comfortable turning down business.

"Can you assure us that you won't take any other orders for those days?" I glanced at the bride, who shifted uncomfortably in her seat and the groom, who wasn't paying attention at all. He slid down further in his chair and crossed his legs. Apparently there was something fascinating on the ceiling because his gaze seemed permanently fixed there.

"I have both those days free," I said. I turned to the bride. "How many servings of cake will you need?"

"I think about a hundred," she said.

"I think not," interrupted the groom's mother. "There will be well over a hundred on Darren's side alone."

"How much does it cost per serving?" the bride asked. The older woman bristled and sat forward in her seat. I don't think she approved of her son's choice of a wife, and I pictured a lifetime of unpleasant family functions. The groom's posture remained unchanged, but he'd refocused his attention to something on the far wall. I wondered what bizarre twist of fate had brought this unlikely pair together.

"Here's how it works—you order your cake, I deliver it, and then I leave you an invoice. Then within a week, you pay whatever you think the cake was worth."

"Yes, but I can only afford three hundred dollars."

"It looks like we'll have to pay for everything," the groom's mother whispered, but it was coarse and loud. The groom was a mute lump between them.

"I don't want you to pay for everything." There was a quiver in the bride's voice. "That's why I'd like to choose a smaller cake."

"We're putting the cake in the foyer, Samantha. The room will swallow up a small cake. It should be appropriately sized for the space."

"Maybe we could put it somewhere else."

"Oh, please! The foyer is perfect," she said to Samantha. "And there simply has to be enough cake to serve all the guests." Then she turned to me. "A small cake won't do. We'll just have to help pay for it. *If* it turns out to be worth more than three hundred, that is." Warning bells clanged in my head, but the look on the bride's face persuaded me to ignore them.

"Would a two-hundred-serving cake be big enough?" I was speaking to the bride, but she wasn't the one who answered.

"That would be closer," the mother-in-law said, "but I really think you should plan more like 250."

"And what style of cake were you hoping for?" I asked.

"Something simple but pretty," the bride said.

"If we're going to be paying for it, I'd like some say on the style of the cake," the older woman said. I was tempted to ask her if she wouldn't like to stand in for the bride at the altar as well. "The cake should make a statement."

The bride surrendered and sat back in her chair.

"Something that speaks of money and class." She was wasting no humility on me.

I suggested a few options that I hoped would satisfy everyone. Both women considered them. The groom remained silent although he did drag his gaze away from the window to glance at the book a time or two.

An eternity later, we finished the order, and I watched them leave. Darren hadn't uttered a single word. He and his mother sat in the front seat of the car, and Samantha sat in the back. I wanted to tell her to make a run for it and never look back.

On the day of Samantha and Darren's wedding, I drove their cake to a mansion on Mercer Island. A man in a uniform buzzed me through a gate and directed me to a side entrance. The white stone structure was so bright in the sunshine that I could barely stand to look at it.

The interior was lavishly decorated. Topiary trees made of pink and white roses lined the foyer. The huge windows let in streams of sunlight that shone blindingly off the marble floor. The cake table was set up in the curve of the giant staircase that filled the right side of the foyer. A blue silk tablecloth flowed out over the floor like waves of water, making the set-up of the cake an athletic event.

I had to admit, the extravagant cake fit the setting. All five tiers were covered in white fondant, with hand-painted gold fondant swags. Gold and silver sugar baubles were clustered on top of each tier. It was definitely the most ornate cake I had ever made. I hoped that it would please Samantha while still fulfilling all of her mother-in-law's requirements. It was making a statement all right. A deafening one.

As I was finishing the setup, a proper housekeeper, in full uniform, announced that she would sign for the cake. I gave her a copy of the invoice, and she disappeared. I took my photos of the cake and sneaked a few shots of the house to show Mom and Kate.

Since I was on Mercer Island, I stopped at Kate and Sam's and offered to watch Izzy while they went out to dinner. We played princess, watched the Wiggles, and fell asleep together on the couch. I didn't think about the cake again or the sad union that was taking place just a few miles away.

Two weeks passed, and still I hadn't received payment. This was the first time I hadn't been paid on time, and I felt a little awkward, but I sent a second invoice. A week later, I received a letter and payment.

Dear Ms. Benson,

The cake was adequate. The service, however, was unacceptable. We were treated rudely at our initial consultation. We appreciate your method of pricing your cakes, as it makes it possible for us to express our dissatisfaction with your service. We hope this might serve as a lesson to you in the future. Your treatment of the family of the bride and groom is of the utmost importance.

Best wishes in the future,

Mrs. Stratman

Inside the envelope was a check for twenty dollars. "Is she serious?" I checked the envelope to see if I'd missed something, but it was empty. I fell back into my chair. Shock quickly gave way to anger. What was she thinking? I'd delivered a masterpiece! I had to tell someone about this slap in my face, so I called Kate.

"I just got stiffed for the first time. You know that incredible cake I delivered to Mercer Island? Well, listen to this," I said, and I read the letter aloud.

"Wow!" she said. "Was it postmarked from the psychiatric ward?"

"Can you believe that? Kate, that cake was beautiful and I worked on it for nearly four days! And I wasn't rude to them. I just tried to let the bride make one little decision. I'd have let the groom help with the choice too, but I don't think he knew how to talk. I can't believe this." I was practically yelling, but this woman's unfairness had me fired up.

"I'm actually not that surprised," Kate said when I'd finished my tirade. "Abby, you were bound to have a jerk sooner or later, and it sounds like you found her."

"I know, but this is crazy! That cake was amazing," I said, finally calming down a little.

"I know. It stinks. But if you're going to set it up the way you have, you have to take the bad with the good. She's saying it wasn't worth much to *her*. I know it isn't fair, but what are you going to do? Just be glad people like her don't come around very often."

I knew she was right. I was still bothered, but my pricing plan was working pretty well overall. Dad had warned me that people would take advantage of me. I had to take the lumps with the sugar.

At the end of the day, I took great comfort in one big thing: I wasn't marrying Darren Stratman. Samantha deserved a lot more pity than me.

Twelve

Balsamic Strawberry Salad Dressing

1 cup balsamic vinegar
1 cup red wine vinegar
5 strawberries, sliced
¼ cup sugar
¼ cup diced red onion
¼ cup chopped fresh parsley
¾ cup olive oil
fresh strawberries for garnishing

Boil balsamic vinegar, red wine vinegar, and strawberries until the mixture is reduced to about ½ cup. Add sugar, onion, and parsley. Simmer for 10–15 minutes and cool. When cooled, gradually whisk in the oil. Serve over fresh greens and garnish with fresh strawberries.

*E*van needed some work done on his farmhouse, so he invited Dane and me to North Bend for a barbecue and a horseback ride up Mount Si.

I hadn't been to Evan's place since May, and I was eager to see the improvements he'd made. The wooden fence that surrounded the fields had a fresh coat of white paint, giving it a proper Kentucky equestrian look. Two horses were grazing in a green pasture close to the fence as we drove up the long driveway.

I introduced Dane to Evan, and in no time they seemed like old friends. I wandered around the barnyard while Evan and Dane discussed the remodeling of the farmhouse. Several horses contentedly munched grain in the large, red barn. It was quiet and peaceful. No wonder Evan loved it here.

"Glad to see you haven't left me." I turned to see a stunning, dark-haired woman come into the barn. Instantly I thought of Audrey Hepburn as I took in her short, nearly black hair, porcelain skin, and huge dark eyes.

Evan walked over to greet the beautiful stranger. "We were just talking shop until you got here." He put his arm around her. "Nicole, this is my sister Abby and her friend, Dane."

"Nice to meet you," I said.

"I'd about decided I was going to have to live with the fact that there weren't many single people in my ward," Evan said, "but a couple of months ago Nicole gave a talk in sacrament meeting." He and Nicole began saddling the horses. "She'd been away at school."

"I was pleasantly surprised to find a new, single man in the ward when I got back," Nicole said.

Soon the horses were saddled, and we were riding across the pasture toward the gate that led to Mount Si. Since I had the least experience with horses, I rode Cozy, a mild-mannered quarter horse.

Evan dismounted and handed Nicole the reins of his horse while he opened the gate. It looked to me like they'd done this a few times before.

The trail was wide and easy. Evan and Nicole led the way. They rode close together, holding each other's attention.

"You didn't know about her?" Dane asked.

"No. Evan never said a word."

"They seem to know each other pretty well."

"I know. I don't think anyone in the family knows she exists."

Late afternoon sun shone through the trees, mottling everything with bright patches of light. The weather was ideal for horseback riding—sunny with a light breeze that seemed to sense when it was getting too warm. As we climbed Mount Si, the air got cooler. A few white, cottony clouds floated lazily above us. We paused at a little clearing and watched a bright yellow hot air balloon lift off the ground in the valley below. The fields made a patchwork quilt dotted with neat houses and barns. I was sad when it was time to go back.

I had the appetite of a cowboy by the time we got to the house and eagerly helped Nicole make a salad with balsamic strawberry dressing while the guys cooked the steaks.

"So how did you meet Evan?" I asked Nicole.

"He called me the day after I spoke in sacrament meeting."

"You must've made quite an impression."

"I've figured that out. In fact, now that I know him better, I'm surprised he called at all. But I'm glad he did." Nicole had a relaxed and easy way about her. I liked her.

"So you're home for the summer?" I asked.

"I just graduated. I'll be teaching math at the high school here in the fall."

"So when is he planning to introduce you to the family?"

"He invited me to come to your last family dinner, but I was at my cousin's wedding in Spokane. He said Dane is coming to the next one. If I came too, we might overwhelm your parents."

After dinner, we played Yahtzee. Dane was on a lucky streak and won three games in a row before the rest of us cried uncle.

It was dark when we said good night. The sky was clear and the stars were dazzling as we got in the car to leave. We drove slowly down the long, white-fenced drive. "Wow," I sighed. "I love Evan's place. He seems so at home here."

"I wonder how much of that is the ranch and how much is Nicole?" he said. "Does it bother you that he didn't tell you about her?"

"No, but it was a surprise. He's always kept things to himself. I don't think he's ever told me about a girlfriend before. Did they seem serious to you?"

"I don't really know them, but it seemed pretty serious to me. Good thing she loves horses."

"Anyone who ends up with Evan is going to have to love horses," I said. "Just like anyone who ends up with me had better like cake."

"I'm a big cake fan myself. Have been for years," Dane said. He put his arm on the back of my seat and played with my hair. After a few miles, he said, "You know, Abby, my family has been wondering when I'm going to bring you around."

"They know about me?" I asked.

"I'm not quite as private as Evan. You think you're up for it?"

"I think I can handle it." I tried to sound calm, but I wondered what he'd told them about me. I felt excited but nervous. "I hope they like me," I said. That sounded pitiful, and I immediately wished I hadn't said it.

"I'm not too worried about that," Dane said. "You have no idea how adorable you are, huh?"

"Oh, come on."

"That's probably a good thing. If you did, you might be hard to live with."

Thirteen

Lemon Cream Cake

1 cup butter, softened
2 cups sugar
3 large eggs
1 tsp. vanilla
2 tsp. grated lemon rind
3½ cups cake flour
2 tsp. baking powder
1 tsp. soda
½ tsp. salt
2 cups sour cream

Spray three (9-inch) round cake pans with cooking spray for baking. Preheat oven to 350°F.

Cream butter and sugar together. Add eggs one at a time, beating after adding each one. Add vanilla and lemon rind. Sift dry ingredients together and add to creamed mixture a little at a time, alternating with the sour cream. Divide batter among the three pans. Bake for 30–35 minutes or until tests done. Cool.

LEMON FILLING

1 can lemon pie filling
⅓ cup sugar
2 large eggs

2 cups milk
1 cup whipping cream
1 tsp. grated lemon peel

Combine pie filling, sugar, and eggs in saucepan. Add milk and cook over medium heat, stirring constantly. Bring to boil. Reduce heat and cook for 5 minutes. Remove from heat. Add lemon peel. Place wax paper over top of pan to cool. Whip cream until soft peaks form. Add lemon mixture to whipped cream (reserve ¾ cup lemon mixture to frost top and side of cake with). Put filling between the layers of cake and frost with reserved part.

*B*usiness steadily increased. By the time I'd been open for three months, I was booking about two cakes per week. I was making pretty good money. Most customers treated me fairly. Except for Mrs. Stratman, of course. I was taking to bakery ownership like a boy band to harmonizing.

I was kneading soft pink coloring into a batch of fondant when the phone rang.

"A Piece of Cake, this is Abby. How can I help you?"

"Yes, hello. My name is Janalee Carver from KTXP Channel 7. May I speak to the owner?"

"I'm the owner," I said. My heart was suddenly racing. Had someone complained about the bakery?

"Oh good. How are you?"

"I'm fine?"

"The reason I'm calling is that we've heard some rumors about your bakery. We've heard that you have an unusual pricing system?"

"Well, I suppose we do."

"So it's true? Do you really let customers pay whatever they want?"

"Actually, I let them pay whatever they think their cake is worth."

"Then it's true! I was sure we'd heard wrong. Wow! So tell me exactly how it works."

I explained to Ms. Carver how the cakes were priced.

"This is just fascinating," she said. "Would it be okay with you if we did a story on your bakery? This is very unusual. I think it would make a great human interest piece."

"I don't know," I said. The idea of being on television was intimidating.

"Well, I've never heard of something like this, and I'll bet most of our viewers haven't either. I think it would make a great story."

I felt torn. The thought of being on television made me a little queasy. But if I did it, most of Seattle would hear about the bakery. "I guess that would be okay."

"Wonderful, can we come tomorrow morning at 10:30?"

"Uh, sure. That would be fine."

I hung up the phone and wondered what I'd just gotten myself into.

"Okay, you need a new outfit. We need to pick up some fresh flowers. What else do we need to do?" Kate started giving me assignments the moment she heard the news. "You do realize that this isn't just a news story. This is a huge TV commercial for your bakery. And it's free."

"I know it is." I was still reeling from the shock. Janalee Carver wanted to interview me. It was crazy. But I would've been happier if I didn't have to appear on TV myself.

"Everything has to look just right."

"Even me," I said.

"Especially you. Abby, you're the face of the bakery."

I cringed.

"I should probably have something for her to taste," I said.

"Ooh, make one of those lemon cream cakes. Those are my favorites."

The next twenty hours were a circus. Kate dropped everything, and an hour later we were sprucing up the shop while the lemon cream cake baked in the oven.

Then we went shopping. Kate insisted we start at Anthropologie. I've always loved window-shopping there, but I'd never had the courage to buy anything. Today was different. Time was running out, and this was for the sake of the business. "Consider this part an advertising expense," she said. The next thing I knew, my free publicity had cost me $250. But now I could appear on camera, respectably dressed in a pin-tucked blouse and rose-appliqued skirt. "This has 'wedding cake shop' written all over it," Kate said. A quick stop at Pike Place for flowers and we were ready.

I knew that the bakery and I were camera ready, but I was so nervous I couldn't catch my breath. I said a short prayer when I saw the KTXP news van pull up. That calmed me down a little.

Janalee was one of the tiniest women I'd ever stood beside. She couldn't have been more than five feet with her heels on. I felt like a giant. Her brunette, shoulder-length hair was heavily sprayed into a proper newswoman style. I resisted the urge to touch it to see if it moved at all. Her makeup looked heavier than on television. I hoped I wouldn't look too washed out next to her.

Janalee walked around the bakery with the cameraman, pointing out things she wanted him to film. She was particularly excited about a dummy cake that looked like bridal lace and encouraged him to get a good close-up shot of the piping. A few minutes later, we were in our chairs talking like old friends. It all happened so smoothly that I forgot it was an interview. The cameraman almost seemed to disappear.

When the interview was over, the cameraman left to set up for an outside shot and Janalee continued to chat with me.

"Your bakery is lovely, and your idea is truly original. I hope this works out well for you," she said.

"Thanks. I hope so too."

"You know, I think you may need to hire some help."

"Maybe someday, if business picks up."

"I'd think about it sooner than later."

On her way out, she turned back. "We'll be airing this on Sunday's 'Around Town' segment. Be sure to set your DVR! Thanks again."

The cameraman filmed Ms. Carver in front of the bakery before they loaded the van and left. It took me about two seconds to call Mom.

This was definitely a Sunday I wanted the family to be together. Then I called Dane.

Sunday, the big day, came. Dane was making his first appearance at family dinner, and I was making my first appearance on television. "Your driver has arrived," Dane said when I opened the front door.

"Cut it out," I said.

"I didn't know I was dating a celebrity." I loved it when he made casual dating references. So many guys were too afraid to say the d-word out loud.

We went to my ward together before we joined the family for dinner and the Sunday evening news.

The joking and teasing started as soon as we walked in the front door. Sam wanted my autograph, and Evan asked if he could be my agent.

"I've got dibs on chauffeur," Dane said.

Dane fit right in with the family. Dad quietly observed everything. He seemed pleased. I caught his eye, and he gave me a little nod.

We ate roasted chicken and baby red potatoes. I'm sure they were good; Mom makes the best roasted chicken on the planet. Unfortunately, I ate without tasting anything. After dinner, we settled into the family room. Dane and Evan were acting like old friends. Evan gave an update on the riding school he was trying to set up. Izzy stared at Dane until he smiled at her, and then she buried her face in Kate's shoulder. This soon developed into a little game. I was enjoying myself so much I almost forgot to be nervous about the interview.

At six o'clock we turned on the television. Dane squeezed my hand. The leading news stories seemed to drag on interminably.

After a commercial break, Brit Michaels, the anchorman, said in his rich baritone: "How would you like to go shopping and be able to set your own prices? Janalee Carver found one Seattle business that lets you do just that. Janalee, what is this all about?"

"Well, Brit, for the last couple of weeks, I've been hearing rumors about a bakery specializing in wedding cakes where the customers can name their own price. I thought it sounded too good to be true, but I decided to check it out. And sure enough, A Piece of Cake does exactly that."

"There's your bakery," Mom said. The camera panned the showroom. Kate squealed.

"I went to A Piece of Cake to see just how the idea works," Janalee said. "I spoke to Abby Benson, the owner, and she told me that it all came about over Sunday dinner with her family."

Then I was on the TV screen. "Abby, you're famous," Evan said.

I looked okay, but wished I'd have worn my hair down. The up-do looked a little severe. But all in all I looked pretty good, and I was glad Kate had convinced me to buy the outfit.

Then I heard myself speak. "I really didn't know what to charge, and I liked the idea of people paying just what they thought it was worth." It made me grimace. I didn't like the way my voice sounded on television.

Janalee continued. "Weren't you afraid people would take advantage of you?"

"There is always that possibility, but overall I've found that people want to be fair. When they're happy with a cake, they usually pay a fair price."

"How do people react when you tell them your pricing system?"

"They're usually pretty surprised, but once I explain how it works, they usually like the idea."

The screen showed a couple of my show cakes. Janalee said, "As you can see, the cakes here at A Piece of Cake are beautiful." Then the camera returned to Janalee, who was just finishing a bite of lemon cream cake. "And you can take my word for it. They taste as good as they look."

The last shot was of Janalee standing out by the sign in front of the bakery, with a display cake in the window behind her. "So, Seattle, if you're in the market for a wedding cake, check out A Piece of Cake— the only bakery I know of where *you* decide what the cake is worth. But just a little warning—your cake might end up being worth more than you can afford to pay. Reporting from A Piece of Cake in West Seattle, I'm Janalee Carver."

Everyone cheered. "You did great," Dane said and kissed my cheek.

"Is that really how I sound?" I asked.

"You were a pro," Dad said. "What great publicity. It couldn't have gone better." The evening turned into a celebration. We ate brownies and vanilla ice cream, and everyone stayed later than usual.

Finally it was time to go home. I felt tired and content on the ride home. My family liked Dane, Dane liked my family, and my business was thriving. And I hadn't made a fool of myself on television. The day couldn't have been better. And then it was.

When Dane kissed me good-bye (several times), I had to admit that life right now was pretty sweet.

Fourteen

Basic Fondant Buttons

cornstarch
fondant
circle cutters
#3 and #5 icing tips

Start by dusting work surface with cornstarch. Set aside a small bowl of cornstarch. You'll want to dip your tools into the corn starch to prevent them from sticking.

Roll your fondant to approximately ¼ inch thick. Using a circle cutter, cut a disc of fondant. Select a smaller circle cutter and gently press into the cut circle, just enough to leave an indentation. Be sure to apply even pressure and don't cut all the way through the fondant.

Dip the icing tip into the corn starch and then press and twist in the center of the fondant disc to create the button holes. You can do two or four holes.

Set finished buttons on a tray or piece of paper to dry. They will dry completely hard in a few hours. They can be stored in an airtight container for several months. When decorating with the fondant buttons, you can use a bit of tinted royal icing to mimic the look of thread.

I slept peacefully the night I was on the news. If I'd known what was coming, I'd have enjoyed it more. Peace was about to abandon me.

The phone was ringing when I walked into the bakery Monday morning. There were thirteen messages already on the answering machine. I began taking and returning calls and soon had a dozen appointments set. But the phone didn't stop ringing. By mid-afternoon, I'd scheduled twenty-two appointments. People were coming from as far away as Everett and Tacoma.

Tuesday was the same. The phone continued to ring. I had to let the machine pick up the calls that came while I was meeting with customers in the afternoon. Dane called twice that afternoon, but both times he only got the machine, and I didn't hear his messages until evening. I called him back but was disappointed when his phone went straight to voice mail.

That night I was exhausted, and I hadn't worked on an actual cake for two days. I breathlessly looked over my appointments. It was hard to believe that just a few months ago, I'd been afraid I wouldn't have any business. Now I wondered how I would handle it all.

I carried a bag of gum paste home with me. I still had dozens of flowers to make for Thursday's cake. I ate a sandwich and then formed orchid petals until after midnight when I fell into bed.

Wednesday the phone calls slowed down a little, but I still had over a dozen calls to return and customer appointments scheduled all afternoon. And I hadn't had a minute to bake the cake for Thursday or make buttons for a cake on Saturday. So I did what every girl in a bind does—I called my mom. Unfortunately, she was at a movie with Dad and didn't get my message until the next day. I tried Kate too, but before I could ask her what she was doing all evening, she told me Izzy had a fever, so I didn't even ask.

I spent most of the night baking the twelve layers that would make up four tall tiers of a chocolate fondant cake with white orchids. But in my overtired state, I made two ten-inch chocolate layers before I realized the ten-inch cake was supposed to be carrot. It took me another weary hour to fix the problem. At last, around four o'clock, I dragged myself home to catch a couple of hours of sleep.

I needed help. But I was too busy to try and get it. A few hours after I'd left the bakery, I was back, assembling and decorating the cake, taking phone calls, and scheduling appointments. For the first time, I was afraid I wasn't going to make my delivery time. I was piping a bead border around one of the cakes when the phone rang. It was Dane.

"How's Seattle's celebrity baker doing?" he asked.

"I'm completely buried. I've got a cake I'm supposed to deliver in two hours and it's not ready yet, I've got appointments most of the day tomorrow, and I haven't even started on the decorations for my Saturday cake."

"Is there anything I can do to help?"

"Not unless you know how to make buttons out of fondant," I said.

"I could give it a try."

For a moment I actually considered it. "You're a sweetheart to offer, but I'll be okay."

"Have you eaten anything today?"

"I haven't had time."

"When can you take a break and eat?"

"I don't think I can. Thanks though."

"Abby, you have to eat. Let's get some dinner after you make your delivery." I was holding the phone between my ear and my shoulder, trying to talk and pipe at the same time.

"I really can't. I've got about a hundred buttons to make, and if tomorrow is anything like the rest of this week, I won't have any time during bakery hours to make them. Sorry."

"That's okay. Have you thought about hiring some help?"

At that moment, my multi-tasking skills failed me, and I realized that the last several beads were smaller than the rest. I sighed and scraped them off.

"Of course I have. But I don't have time. The phone rings all day, and I barely have time to bake, let alone interview people."

"I won't keep you, then. Just let me know if I can do anything to help."

Then I realized how short I was being, and I felt terrible. I laid down the piping bag and massaged the headache above my eyes.

"I'm sorry, Dane. I know you're trying to help. I wish I had time to go eat with you or even just to talk on the phone, but I'm just so swamped."

"Don't worry about it. I'll check in with you later." I hung up and finished the cake. After I'd safely delivered it to the Pierpont Hotel, I got a drive-thru hamburger and ate it on my way back to the bakery, where I made buttons for several more hours.

I was exhausted. I hadn't had enough sleep all week, and I was losing control of everything. I looked at the buttons I'd made. I looked at the order form for my next cake. I had appointments starting in less than an hour, and the phone was already ringing. I had to get control. I let the answering machine catch a few calls and dialed the number for You're Hired Employment Agency. LouAnn, the employment specialist, said she'd send over someone to answer the phones within a few hours. Someone with baking experience would take some time, but she'd start looking for someone right away.

I was relieved. I'd get some help, get this awful week behind me, and things would be okay.

I was with a customer picking out cake flavors when the bell rang. I looked up to see a female Marilyn Manson walk through the door. "LouAnn said you needed my help," she said.

"Hi. Could you just wait right there at the desk? I'll be with you in a minute."

"Sure thing." She tromped over to the desk, her combat boots echoing through the room. Her skirt was a foot too short and her fishnet stockings were torn and ragged.

The phone rang almost immediately. "You want me to get that?" she asked.

"No thanks. The machine will pick it up."

A couple of minutes later, the customer left, and I introduced myself to the new girl.

"I'm Dekay. That's d-e-k-a-y."

"Hi. I'm Abby."

"That's not my real name, but that's what all my friends call me. I'm thinking of having it legally changed. It's all about the condition of being, you know. Nothing stays the same. Plants decay, societies decays. We're decaying right now. Pretty soon there's nothing left. Just poof. We're gone. My boyfriend likes it so much he got it tattooed on his chest—right across his heart." I wasn't sure what to say.

"Did LouAnn tell you what you'd be doing for me?" I asked.

"She said you needed somebody to answer phones and greet customers."

"Right." Had LouAnn actually met Dekay? I could barely tear my eyes away from the scab around what looked to be an infected lip piercing.

The phone rang. Before I could stop her she'd picked up the receiver. "Hello. This is . . ." She looked suddenly flustered. Then she cursed into the phone. "I'm new here and I just realized I don't know the name of this place. But can I help you?" I flinched. "Just a minute."

I didn't have time to spend training someone I knew wasn't going to work out, so I wrote the name of the bakery on a piece of paper, handed it to her, and told her to just take down phone numbers. I'd call them back myself. Then I went into the kitchen and baked cakes. As soon as Dekay had gone for the day, I called LouAnn and told her she wasn't going to work out.

So there I was, back where I started with no one to help me. The funny thing was that part of me was thrilled at this increase in business. Unfortunately it was killing me.

I delivered the cake on Saturday, and as soon as church was over on Sunday, I went to the bakery and wrote out the next week's schedule. It was scary. I called my mom, and she agreed to answer the phone for a couple of days until I got some help.

Mom saved my bacon. She answered phones and scheduled appointments all the next week. On Thursday, LouAnn sent over April, and Mom helped me train her. She was a waif of a girl with intense blue eyes, dark hair, and an easy smile. Soon she was settled at the desk in the showroom and was taking calls. Now I just needed someone to help out in the kitchen.

After a few more days, Trina came to interview for the kitchen position. I liked her immediately. I liked her even better when she told me she'd worked in a bakery all through high school. I showed her around the kitchen and taught her how to make fondant daisies. She spent the rest of the day forming lovely little flowers. After the week I'd just suffered through, I felt like I wanted to sing.

I was stunned when LouAnn called the next morning and told me that Trina thought the job was too boring and wouldn't be coming back. She said she'd try to find someone to replace her as soon as she could.

When I glanced at the clock just after eight, I still had hours to go on the next day's cake. It looked like it would be another all-nighter. Someone knocked on the front door of the bakery. "I'm closed," I said under my breath. They knocked again and I'd had it. I stormed into the showroom and shouted, "I'm closed." Then I saw it was Dane.

"What are you doing here?" I asked.

"I had a feeling you weren't eating again." He held up a bag. "I hope you're in the mood for Mexican."

"Mexican sounds great." I pulled him down and kissed him and got flour in his hair.

We ate and Dane kept me company until I finished a few hours later. I was still exhausted, but the time practically flew by, and I suddenly realized how much I'd really missed him.

I'd interviewed three other girls before Lara arrived. She had no experience in a bakery, but she was enthusiastic and seemed ready for anything. She was a sturdy, athletic girl who had played college softball and wore her hair in a simple ponytail. I showed her how to make fondant roses, and by the time I started my appointments a couple of hours later, she was making them on her own.

The next day we let the machine pick up the phones, ordered lunch, and had our first staff meeting. I'd attended staff meetings before, but I'd never been in charge of one. At first I felt strange, like a kid playing "office" with her friends, but after a while I got the hang of it.

We sat around the desk with a calendar and some notebooks, and together we came up with ways to manage this onslaught of business. "Scheduling has never really been a problem before, but the volume of calls and orders has increased dramatically. We need a good system or we're going to miss something important. And when you're dealing with wedding cakes, the smallest mistake is a catastrophe."

By the end of the meeting, we'd established some protocols I hoped would help us manage the workload. That afternoon, I called for a new phone line, and by the end of the week, we were wired with three phone lines and an intercom system.

April and Lara were hardworking and excited to be involved in something so creative and romantic. After a few weeks, I realized they were worth more than I was paying them, so I gave them a raise. I realized it was important to me that I pay what I thought they were worth. How could I hope to be treated fairly by my customers if I wasn't fair with my employees?

Fifteen

Chocolate Chip Cookie Pie

2 eggs
½ cup flour
½ cup sugar
½ cup brown sugar
1 cup butter, melted and cooled
1 cup semisweet chocolate chips
1 cup chopped pecans or walnuts
1 (9-inch) unbaked pie shell

Preheat oven to 325°F. In large bowl, beat eggs until foamy. Add flour and both sugars. Beat until well blended and blend in melted butter. Stir in chocolate chips and nuts. Pour into pie shell. Bake for 55–60 minutes. Serve with ice cream.

I must have looked shell-shocked as we walked to the front door of Dane's parents' house. Dane gave my shoulder a reassuring squeeze. "It'll be fine," he said. I was surprised at how ordinary the house looked. Since Dane's dad was a builder, I'd expected something new and showy, not a thirty-year-old rambler.

The inside of the house was a surprise. It felt like a brand new house when we walked through the front door. Soft colors, overstuffed furniture, and a few purposely placed antiques created a charm I'd have never expected from the exterior. I loved it.

"I thought I heard someone come in," Dane's mom said. Mrs. Reynolds was a sturdy, friendly woman with a quick smile, short graying hair, and Dane's green eyes. "You must be Abby. It's so nice to meet you."

She led us through the wide entry hall and into the living room. Mr. Reynolds, a man even taller than Dane, shook my hand. He had a build like a lumberjack and a face like Cary Grant. Blake and his wife, Sarah, said hello and made a spot for Dane and me to sit together. Blake was shorter and huskier than Dane. In fact, he and Sarah were about the same height. She had a short, messy haircut that declared self-confidence.

"The kids are downstairs. You can meet them when we call them up for dinner," Sarah said.

"Just make yourselves at home. Dinner will be ready soon," Mrs. Reynolds said.

We asked and answered the usual getting-to-know-you questions until a beeping sound came from the kitchen. "There's dinner. Shall we eat?" Mrs. Reynolds led the way. Two little towheads, a boy and a girl, raced into the dining room. They stopped abruptly when they saw me.

"Ruby and Benjamin, this is Abby, Uncle Dane's friend," Sarah said.

I was soon forgotten as they tussled over who got to sit beside Dane. Ruby won because she was older and Sarah needed to be able to cut up Benjamin's meat.

"So, Abby, are your parents from around here?" Mr. Reynolds asked.

"My mom was raised in Marysville and Dad is from Bend, Oregon, but they decided to settle up here after he graduated from college. They've lived in Bellevue for about thirty years. Are you from here?"

"My family has been here for three generations," Mrs. Reynolds said. "Hal was born in Colorado, but his family moved here when he was six, so he's only been here about a hundred years."

"Some days it feels that long," Mr. Reynolds said.

"We watched you make your television debut," Sarah said. "That must've been exciting."

"I was scared to death."

"Some of those cakes were fantastic. I wish you'd been around when we got married. Our cake was awful. It was so lopsided I thought it was going to tip over," Sarah said.

"Our cake looked fine, but you should have tasted it," Mrs. Reynolds said. "The baker said we had to have fruitcake so it would be sturdy. Fruitcake! I don't think anyone ate a single bite."

"We didn't even feed each other a piece," said Mr. Reynolds. "We just stood there holding it for the picture. There was no way I was going to eat it."

"I was wondering what you could possibly see in Dane," Blake said, "but after seeing you on TV, I figured it out. You need a bodyguard. He's a little skinny, but I'll bet he can hold his own with the monster brides."

"Or the monster mother-in-laws," I said. Everyone at the table glanced uncomfortably at Mrs. Reynolds, and I felt my face flush. "Oh no. Not you," I said. I told the story of the twenty-dollar cake and everyone was properly appalled.

I enjoyed listening to Dane and Blake joke with each other. It was easy to see that they were good friends as well as brothers. Before the meal was over, Blake was teasing me like I was one of the family, and I almost felt like I was.

"Let's do the dishes," I said to Dane. He nodded.

"We'll be in the kitchen washing dishes, if you need us," Dane said.

"We can help," Sarah said.

"That's okay. We've got it covered," Dane said, and I saw him give a little wink.

Soon we were alone washing dishes. "I can tell they like you. Blake doesn't tease anyone he doesn't like," Dane said.

"I like them too."

When the dishes were done, Dane pulled me close, linking his hands behind my back. Then he kissed me. I was surprised by the suddenness and intensity of the kiss.

He stroked my hair. "Thanks for coming."

I wanted to stay like that forever. He smelled so good, and his arms felt so nice. "We'd better get in there," I said, but I didn't move.

"I guess we'd better." He didn't move either. Finally he sighed and took my hand. "Let's go."

The rest of the family was watching a home improvement show. They chatted as they watched, commenting on things they liked or ways they'd do it better.

I excused myself to go to ladies' room. When I returned, I paused in the hall and looked at the family pictures that filled the wall. There were pictures of Dane and Blake playing T-ball, photographs of high school dances, and pictures taken in front of the MTC. There was Blake and Sarah's wedding and a formal family portrait that included Sarah and the children. As I looked at the wall of family history, I could hear the hushed conversation taking place in the living room.

"She seems like a very nice girl," Mrs. Reynolds said.

"She *is*," said Dane.

"She's not like Jessica at all," Sarah said. "I wouldn't have thought she was your type, but I really like her."

I stopped in my tracks. Who was Jessica?

"I didn't know I had a type," Dane said.

"You know," Blake said. "You usually date girls who are tall and blonde. How tall was Jessica? She had to be five-foot-eleven. Abby's different."

"I don't think you've ever dated anyone with freckles before," Sarah said. I put my hands up to my burning, freckled cheeks.

"I think she's great," said Mr. Reynolds. "She seems like a real sweet girl with her head on straight. That's what you want."

"I like her," Dane said. "A lot. And I like her freckles." I couldn't walk into the room now. I stood there trying to make sense of what I'd heard.

Tall. Blonde. Jessica. I took a deep breath. I didn't want them to know I'd overheard the conversation. I slipped back into the bathroom and waited a minute for my heart to stop racing. When I walked out the second time, I closed the door loudly enough for them to hear it.

There was an awkward feeling in the room when I came back, and I noticed a couple of uncomfortable glances.

"There are some great pictures in the hall," I said. "It's nice when family photos are on display and not just hidden away in albums." It felt as if the room let out a sigh of relief, and I congratulated myself on easing the tension. As soon as I sat down, Dane took my hand and held it. I felt his eyes on me, but I couldn't look at him. I was afraid he'd be able to tell I'd heard everything.

"We should probably get going," Dane said.

"Oh, you can't leave yet." Mrs. Reynolds was already walking to the kitchen. "I made chocolate chip cookie pie. It's Dane's favorite."

"I'll help you," I said.

Mrs. Reynolds sliced the pie, and I put a scoop of vanilla ice cream on top of each piece.

"Dane has been very happy since he met you," Mrs. Reynolds said.

"I've been pretty happy myself."

"It seems like your life has been awfully hectic since you two met."

"I know. It's hard to believe everything that's happened in the last six months."

"Do you think it will settle down soon?" She sounded friendly, but I had the feeling there were a hundred other questions lurking beneath the surface of that one. Did I sense a little disapproval from her?

"I'm sure it will. I've hired some help, so hopefully that will keep things manageable."

"That's good," she said. I couldn't tell if she really thought that was good or if she had more she wanted to say. It felt like something was hanging unspoken in the air.

It only took one bite to see why this pie was Dane's favorite. I'd have liked a second piece. In fact I'd have liked an entire pie.

We left a short time later. Dane and I didn't speak on the way to the truck or even after we were buckled up and driving away. At the corner, Dane took a turn that led away from my house. He seemed to have something on his mind. I didn't dare ask what he was thinking about. Was he remembering Jessica? Was he realizing I was too short and dark-haired and freckled? I wasn't sure if I wanted to know, so I said nothing.

A few minutes later, we pulled into the driveway of a craftsman home with a wide wrap-around porch. It was dark. Dane turned off the ignition and faced me.

"Want to come in for a few minutes?" he asked.

"This is your house?"

"Yeah. I thought maybe you'd like to see it. We can save it for another time if you're too tired. I just thought since we were so close, I'd drive you by."

"It looks nice," I said.

"It wasn't so nice when I bought it two years ago. But I knew it had potential."

"I'd love to see it," I said.

It was a man's house, but I liked it. Everything was big and solid and natural with dark hardwood floors and rich woodwork in all directions. A braided rug runner ran up the middle of the stairs, held in place with copper rods. The dark wood handrail curved into nearly a full circle at the bottom of the stairs. The rooms were big and open. A slate fireplace filled the wall of the family room. The furniture was simple and masculine.

Dane showed me around each room and pointed out the details—the bathroom walls he'd peeled four layers of wallpaper from, the crown molding he'd stripped and stained, and the balusters he'd made to match the originals. The craftsmanship was excellent, and some of the details reminded me of my antique door.

Finally, Dane led me down a tiled hall to the kitchen, a tidy and practically laid-out room with an attached dining room.

"I knocked out the wall here to make one big room. Before I did, the kitchen felt like a phone booth, and I didn't like to be in here much. Now, I actually don't mind cooking." I pictured us cooking here together and then stopped myself.

"This old farm sink is the first thing I ever bought from Annie," he said.

I sat on a bar stool at the counter, and Dane made hot chocolate—with little marshmallows.

"So that was nice of you to mention the pictures in the hall when you walked back in the room." He watched my reaction. "You heard, didn't you?"

"Yes," I said.

"I'm sorry."

"It's all right."

"No, it's not. It must've been uncomfortable for you."

I didn't know what to say. I didn't want to appear insecure by asking too many questions about a past girlfriend, especially one he'd never mentioned before. But I was dying to know more.

I didn't look at him. I stirred in the marshmallows and then took a sip of hot cocoa.

"It wasn't really a big deal," he said.

"Your entire family was talking about her. It seems like it might have been a big deal."

"We quit dating before I even met you."

I buried my hands in my pockets. "Were you two serious?"

"Yeah, I guess we were."

"What happened?"

"We didn't want the same things, so we split up."

I almost held my breath. "Would you still be with her if you'd had the same priorities?"

"Maybe. But it doesn't matter anymore."

"Sorry. This isn't fair. I guess . . . I guess I just heard more than I wanted to."

"Listen, Abby. I'm glad it didn't work out."

I watched the marshmallows melt in my hot cocoa. "It sounds like she was really pretty."

"She wasn't prettier than you. The longer I knew her, the less pretty she became to me. You're just the opposite. You get prettier the more I know you." Dane's eyes got big. "No. I didn't mean . . . That's not what I meant to say. Of course I thought you were pretty the first time I saw you. It's just . . ."

"It's okay," I said.

"Abby, I didn't think you were ugly." He slapped his head. "Aw, just shoot me."

"It's okay." I walked over to him, stood on my tiptoes, and kissed him.

"I'm such an idiot."

"Just go back to the part about me being pretty," I said.

He put his arms around me. "Look, Abby. I like you a lot. I'm sorry about tonight. I'd rather lose an arm than make you feel bad." By the look on his face, I think he meant it.

I linked my hands behind his neck. "Families talk. I'm sure they didn't mean anything by it." I pulled him down and kissed him on the lips. "Besides, there's really only one Reynolds I'm trying to impress."

Sixteen

Maple Crème Brûlée

1 vanilla bean
1 qt. heavy cream
½ cup sugar
8 egg yolks
⅓ cup pure maple syrup

Preheat oven to 350°F. Split vanilla bean down center and scrape seeds into a large pot with the cream and sugar. Add the vanilla pod to the pot. While stirring, heat cream mixture on medium heat until it just starts to bubble. Remove from heat and remove vanilla pod. Whisk egg yolks and maple syrup together. Slowly add hot cream to egg mixture.

Pour equal amounts of custard mixture into eight 6-ounce ramekins (custard cups). Place ramekins in a baking pan and fill pan with warm water halfway up the sides of ramekins.

Bake for 45 minutes, until custard is set. Custard will be mostly firm but will still jiggle slightly in the center. Remove from water bath and cool in refrigerator overnight.

Just before serving, sprinkle top of each custard dish evenly with brown sugar and place under broiler until sugar becomes a golden brown.

*L*ara and April were working out well, and life seemed to be under control again. Mondays were pretty slow at the bakery, so on a Monday in September, Dane took the day off, and we caught the earliest ferry to Victoria, B.C. We ate French toast on the boat and planned our day with the help of a few tourist pamphlets.

Fitting in time for real dating had become a challenge. To have a whole day together was a rare luxury, and I was more than a little excited at the prospect.

The ferry pulled into Victoria beside the large cruise ships. The stately buildings and elegant architecture made it feel like we were arriving in old-world Europe instead of a modern Canadian city. We found a kiosk selling tours, and soon we boarded a double-decker bus. In spite of the cool morning weather, we sat on the open-air top deck.

We snuggled under a blanket and listened as the tour guide described various sites and their history. Baskets of brightly colored flowers hung from lampposts. I had to resist the urge to reach out and touch the flowers as we passed under them. The day warmed up quickly, and soon we shed the blanket and our jackets.

We toured the miniature museum with its tiny dioramas and sculptures of wee little people. Dane liked the Canadian Railroads, but I was fascinated by London. Then we came across a first-grade class at the circus display and had as much fun watching the children as we did looking at the display.

Craigdarroch Castle was a half-hour walk from the museum, so we followed the tourist map and strolled through the neatly manicured neighborhoods to the mansion. The castle was situated on large, manicured grounds and loomed over the surrounding homes. Donovan, our guide, explained that a wealthy coal baron, Robert Dunsmuir, had built the home as a demonstration of his love for his wife.

We admired the stained glass and intricately carved woodwork. We climbed the eighty-seven steps to the top of the tower where we looked out over what Donovan assured us was the best view of Victoria in all of the city. We weren't disappointed. The distant water was crystal blue, with each wave sparkling like diamonds in the sunshine. The buildings in the city below looked like they'd been built for the sole purpose of providing this breathtaking vista.

In the parlor, Donovan pointed out a light fixture that had been imported from Italy, marble from somewhere in Asia, and a tapestry from Turkey. He pointed out the parts of the house that had been used as the March's home in *Little Women* and pulled out a picture of Winona Ryder and Christian Bale standing in front of the castle. We finished the tour in a little gift shop where they sold postcards for ten times their downtown price.

It was hot as we walked back from the castle, and I was grateful for the breeze that came up off the Strait of Juan de Fuca.

"It must've been nice to be able to do something like that for his wife," Dane said.

"Not many husbands could build their wives a home like that," I said. "It's a good thing there are more affordable ways of showing love."

"I'm not sure the expensive gestures necessarily show love anyway. Maybe the house was more about *looking* like he loved her than actually loving her."

"I wouldn't even want the big fancy house without real love," I said. "I think you can tell more by the little everyday things than the extravagant ones."

"What everyday things do you think are important?"

"I'd want him to be a good friend. I guess a husband who's helpful and interested in what I'm doing and who loves me and considers my feelings. I think the same would be true of a wife. What do you think?"

Dane was thoughtful for a moment. "I think the most important thing is to put each other first. That tells you what you're worth to each other." There it was again—that word *worth*.

"I've never thought so much about the word *worth* before," I said. "Something can have a totally different value for different people. Like the wedding cakes. For some people it's a nice part of the wedding and they're glad to have it, but if they didn't have it, it wouldn't be the end of the world. Those people pay a fair amount, but you can tell that the wedding cake wasn't really that important to them. But for some the cake really matters. It symbolizes the day so perfectly that they're willing to pay a lot."

Dane nodded. "I guess the same is true with people. If a person is worth a lot to you, you'd do a lot to show them."

"Like give of your time and make sacrifices and be kind." I said. "I want my husband to value me enough that he's willing to put out some effort. And I plan to do the same for my husband." I felt a twinge of guilt as I recognized the hypocrisy of my words. Dane was important to me, but so many times lately I'd put the bakery before him. But then we weren't married, and I had to put the time into the bakery or it would fail. Things wouldn't always be like this.

We ate dinner at Chandler's Seafood House, a little restaurant a few blocks from the pier. We ate slowly, enjoying the delicious food, the elegant atmosphere, and the soft music. We shared a maple crème brûlée and then walked back to the ferry holding hands.

On the boat, we found a cushioned window seat. Dane stretched out with a leg on the seat. I sat with my back against him, and he put his arms around me. The sky turned a velvety black as we watched the lights of Victoria disappear into the distance. We didn't talk much. At one point we both fell asleep, and when I woke up, I could see the familiar Seattle skyline.

We walked slowly from the ferry to Dane's truck, and he took an unnecessarily long route to my house. The day had been a much-needed respite from the frenzy of real life, and we were reluctant for it to end.

In the driveway Dane turned and looked at me. Several electric seconds passed in silence, and I began to feel self-conscious. "What are you thinking?" I asked.

He started to speak and then stopped. I waited. Finally he said, "I had a great day today."

"Me too."

He was quiet again. Time stood still. It seemed like there was more he wanted to say. I'd never seen him so uncomfortable.

"Is everything okay?" I asked.

He laughed awkwardly. "I just . . . you're amazing. That's all."

"Thank you," I said. "So are you."

I think he felt a little silly about the whole exchange, because at that point he quickly got out of the truck and walked me to the porch. He kissed me and held me close for a long time. Then without another word, he left.

Usually a date ending like this would have thrown me into a dither. Had I done something wrong? Why had he left so abruptly? Why had he been so quiet? But for some reason, I wasn't worried. Dane had been speechless. Because of me. It felt pretty good.

Seventeen

A Fairy Tale Day

a long boat ride
a boy you're falling for
a castle
a delicious meal

Combine all ingredients. Add good conversation, smiles, and holding hands. Top off with an amazing kiss and a hug that ends too soon. Enjoy the day over and over, remembering every detail as you fall asleep. Try to resist the temptation to add "and they lived happily ever after."

"Abby, is that you?" April said from her desk as I walked in the back door.

"I'll be right there." I stopped in my office and jotted a couple of items on my list for the day. When I looked up, April was standing in the doorway waving a message slip above her head. "Is everything okay?" I asked.

"It's a good thing you showed up. I was about to come back to your house to get you. You're not going to believe this message." She was practically jumping up and down. I reached for the slip of paper. At first I didn't see what was so exciting. Someone named Melissa had called. The number had a 212 area code. And then I saw it.

"She's from *The Today Show*?"

"Can you believe it?" April was practically shrieking. "She wants you to call her back."

"Did she say what she wants?"

"No. She wanted to talk to you. What are you waiting for? Call her right now! I told her you'd be in any minute."

"I can't call her yet. I can hardly breathe." My head was spinning, and a knot the size of a basketball had formed in my stomach. Did *The Today Show* want to talk to me about my bakery? I had to get myself under control. If I called now, I'd probably make a fool of myself. I sat down in my chair, laid the paper on my desk, and smoothed out the message. Then I picked up the phone and called Kate.

"Kate, you're not going to believe this. Someone from *The Today Show* called this morning."

Kate screamed. "Are you serious? Why?"

"I don't know. I wasn't here, and I haven't called them back yet."

"Well, what's wrong with you? *Call them!*"

"I can't until I calm down. I can hardly breathe, let alone call and sound normal."

"Okay, then start calming down!" It was ironic that she was scream-ing at me to calm down.

"Yeah, well you're not helping me."

"It's *The Today Show*, for goodness sake. What do you think they want?"

"I have no idea."

"Go right now. Take a walk around the block and get yourself together and then call them back."

"Okay."

"But walk fast!"

"I will."

"And then call me back immediately. I'm going to be going crazy."

"Okay."

"Go!"

"I'm going."

I stood up on slightly shaky legs and walked to the showroom where April was sharing the morning's news with Lara. She stopped mid-sentence and turned to me. "Did you call?"

"Not yet. I'm going for a walk first. I'll be back in a few minutes and then I'll call."

Lara shooed me out the door. "Hurry up, we're going crazy here." I turned left and walked, my thoughts focused on even breathing and a slower heart rate. The cool, autumn air made goose bumps rise on my bare arms, and I folded my arms and rubbed them as I walked. I was cold but clear-headed when I got back to the shop a few minutes later.

I slowly dialed the number.

"Today Show Studios, how may I direct your call?"

"Melissa Davenport, please."

"May I tell her who's calling?"

"Abby Benson. I'm returning her call."

"One moment please."

A few seconds later, a woman's voice came on the line. "Abby, thanks for calling me back."

"You're welcome."

"I'm a segment producer for *The Today Show*, and we've heard some interesting things about your business. I was hoping I could ask you a few questions so I can see if your story would work for a segment we're doing about unique ways women approach business."

"That would be fine," I said.

"We could do it now if you have a few minutes."

"Now would be fine," I said.

The next ten minutes we talked about the bakery. She asked questions about my pricing policies, past customers, and much more.

"This is a fascinating story," she said. "I think it would fit in nicely with our series. What you've done is really gutsy. Would you be interested in being a guest on the show?"

Fleeting thoughts ran through my mind of the chaos that followed my last interview, but I put them out of my head. "Well, sure, I guess I could be on the show."

"Great! We'll get back with you on the details. Keep any letters or notes you've received. And maybe you could jot down any interesting things you think of. We'll handle part of the prep work over the phone, and we'll send a local crew over to shoot some footage. Then we'll fly you out for the taping of the show."

"Okay."

"Thanks for calling me back, Abby. It's really nice to talk to you."

Shocked, I hung up the phone and sat back in my chair. Lara and April nearly fell into the room.

"Thanks for the privacy," I said.

"Who cares about privacy?" Lara said.

"Details," April said. "We need details."

I figured they knew most of it already, but I gave them a quick rundown anyway before I banished them from the office and called Kate. Then I called Mom and Dad, Evan, and Dane.

That afternoon, my mind was in New York City as my hands cut and painted little fondant squares for a mosaic tile cake.

Eighteen

Corn Tortillas

1¾ cups masa harina (corn flour)
1⅛ cups water

In a medium bowl, mix together masa harina and hot water until thoroughly combined. Turn dough onto a clean surface and knead until pliable and smooth. If dough is too sticky, add more masa harina; if it begins to dry out, sprinkle with water. Cover dough tightly with plastic wrap and allow to stand for 30 minutes.

Preheat a cast-iron skillet or griddle to medium-high.

Divide dough into 15 equal-sized balls. Using a tortilla press, a rolling pin, or your hands, press each ball of dough flat between two sheets of plastic wrap.

Immediately place tortilla in preheated pan and allow to cook for approximately 30 seconds, or until browned and slightly puffy. Turn tortilla over to brown on second side for approximately 30 seconds more and then transfer to a plate. Repeat process with each ball of dough. Keep tortillas covered with a towel to stay warm and moist until ready to serve.

*A*n early morning glow lit the eastern sky as Kate and I boarded the airplane bound for the Big Apple. I'd been to New York with Aunt

Grace as a teenager, but this was Kate's first trip to the East Coast. She was so excited that it hadn't been hard to talk Sam into taking a couple of days off work to be with Izzy.

We stowed our carry-ons, and I fell into my seat, glad for a few hours of quiet. A whirlwind of preparations over the last two weeks had left me worn out. Last week, a television crew had come and filmed the showroom, some outside shots, and me decorating a cake. I could pipe a shell border in my sleep, but doing it in front of the camera made me so jittery they'd had to film four takes.

"What are you going to wear?" Kate had asked.

"I thought I'd wear the same thing I wore last time I was on TV. I looked okay in that."

"No way, Abby. You can't wear the same thing. People will think that's the only nice thing you own."

So Kate and Mom had taken me shopping for an outfit worthy of national television. Shopping for *The Today Show* was much more intimidating than shopping for a local news story. I spent the better part of two days changing clothes and modeling for Mom and Kate. I was so fed up with trying on clothes that weren't quite right, I was about to put my foot down and insist on wearing something I already owned. But then I tried on a steel-blue silk blouse and a black pencil skirt, and I knew the hunt was over. The blouse had tiny ruffle details and three-quarter-length sleeves. I'd never felt fabric so soft and silky before. I added a pair of black boots and hardly recognized the stylish, professional woman who stood there in the mirror. It was the most sophisticated outfit I'd ever worn, and I felt grown up and professional.

I had one cake order that was due the day after I got back, so Lara would do the baking while I was gone, and we'd assemble and deliver it the day after I returned. Everything was in order.

I leaned my head back and closed my eyes. I could hear Kate as she flipped through a magazine. I knew it was pointless to take out the novel I'd bought to read on the plane. I had too much to think about. I hoped Kate would think I was asleep so I could think about the events of the previous evening without interruption.

Dane had called yesterday morning. "Do you have time for me to take you to dinner tonight?"

"I'll make time," I had said. I would need to finish my packing early so I wouldn't have to worry about it that night.

"I'll pick you up at six."

I packed that afternoon. I put the folder of notes and letters from customers in the top of my carry-on and placed both bags by the front door.

I carefully chose what I would wear to dinner. I picked a pair of brown slacks and a cream cashmere sweater with a large, cowl collar and brown, low-heeled ankle boots. Time had been so scarce that I hadn't seen Dane all week, and I wanted to look nice.

"You look beautiful," he said at the front door. "I like your hair." I had had it trimmed with a few more layers cut in, which made my usually unruly hair wavy and more stylish. "Do you have a jacket you can bring?" he asked. It didn't feel cold, but I grabbed one anyway.

The relaxed evening was just what I needed to soothe my frayed nerves. We ate at Cactus on Alki Beach. They seated us at a table by the huge fireplace. The warmth of the fire and the easy conversation were comforting, and I forgot how nervous I was about the next couple of days.

We ordered sizzling fajitas with amazing homemade corn tortillas. Dane chose steak, I picked the prawns, and we shared. It may have been the warm, firelit atmosphere, or it could have been that I was leaving, but we'd never felt so completely at ease together. Being with Dane felt so calm and safe. I wanted to soak in that feeling and take it with me to New York.

When we left the restaurant, Dane opened the car door, but instead of letting me in, he reached in and grabbed our jackets. "Let's go for a walk down by the beach." We crossed Alki Street to the wide paved path that followed the shore of Puget Sound. We held hands as we walked in silence.

Finally Dane spoke. "Are you nervous?"

"Only when I think about it," I said. "I don't know what to expect. Melissa's asked me all the questions she says Matt Lauer will ask, and I have the answers ready. I just hope I don't get stage fright."

"Just remember how well you did here. You'll do fine," he said.

"Yes, but here it was the Sunday evening news without an audience. There it's going to be *The Today Show*, in their studio with people looking in the windows making faces. And millions of people will be watching. It *feels* very different."

"Just enjoy the experience. Most people will never have a chance like this. Try not to let your worries spoil it for you. Just have fun."

"I'll try."

The air was warm and unusually still. Lights sparkled on the water from a few boats floating silently in the sound. The path curved away from Alki Street, and soon the cars were background noise and we could hear the water lapping softly against the rocks on the beach. Dane felt close and protective, and I felt happy.

Before long we reached a small cluster of picnic tables and benches and sat down on the bench nearest the water. We watched a small motorboat rumble by, sending waves lapping faster against the shore. Dane put both his arms around me and held me close, resting his cheek against my hair as we both looked out at the water. A spell had settled over us, and it seemed neither of us wanted to break it.

At last Dane interrupted the silence. "What are you thinking about?"

"How happy I am," I said, and I didn't even feel self-conscious about how sappy that sounded. "What about you?"

"How much I love you," he said without missing a beat. Stunned, I held perfectly still, looking out at the water, replaying in my mind the words he'd just said. "I'm not trying to freak you out or anything. I just wanted you to know that before you left. I want you to leave knowing how I feel."

It took me a minute to catch my breath. I pulled his arms tighter around me. "I love you too," I said. I could feel the stubble on his cheek as he nudged my hair aside and kissed my temple. Neither of us moved. I was touched by this sweet gesture and stunned that he sensed what I needed. Somehow he'd known that this whole trip would be easier if I knew I had someone waiting for me—someone who loved me. A future to look forward to no matter how this trip turned out. I felt incredibly lucky.

A few minutes later, a light sprinkling of raindrops began to fall. We stood to go, and I impulsively reached out and hugged him. He leaned down and kissed me. The rain came a little faster. I'm not sure if it was because the kiss followed that declaration, or if it was because of the rain, but it was the most amazing kiss I'd ever had. My head was spinning, and when we started walking back to the car, I held onto him, not just because I wanted to, but because I needed to in order to keep my balance.

At the car, he took my face in his hands and kissed me again. We didn't talk on the way home. He just held my hand and then kissed it, making my heart melt and race at the same time.

"You and Kate have fun," he said at my front door. "No worrying. About anything."

"No worrying," I said. "But I'll miss you while I'm gone."

"I miss you already." He kissed my nose and then my lips. "Now, go get some sleep."

"I think that might be hard," I said. He squeezed my hand and turned to go, but I pulled him back and kissed him again.

"I have to go, Abby."

"I know."

"And I should probably go now," he said. He pulled away and walked to his car.

I thought I would stay awake replaying the entire evening over and over in my mind. We loved each other. We had said the words. Instead, I surprised myself by falling sound asleep as soon as I pulled the covers up.

⸻❦⸻

Now on the plane, I relived the evening over and over. Dane loved me. He'd wanted me to know before I set out to face the scary unknown. He knew me so well.

I felt someone looking at me, so I opened my eyes. Kate was grinning. I hadn't fooled her at all. She knew I wasn't sleeping, and her mischievous grin told me she probably knew what I was daydreaming about.

Nineteen

Banana and Papaya Smoothie

1 cup milk
½ cup sliced and peeled banana
½ cup chopped, seeded, and peeled papaya
1 Tbsp. honey
½ cup crushed ice

Purée all ingredients in a blender. Pour into a large glass and enjoy!

The plane arrived in New York just after three in the afternoon. We gathered our luggage and made our way down the escalator.

"Oh my goodness, Abby. Is that for you?" said Kate. A uniformed man at the bottom of the escalator was holding a sign that said "Benson."

I stifled a giggle as I approached the man and said, "I'm Abby Benson." He ceremoniously tucked the sign under his arm, took a bag in each hand, and led the way to a limousine that was parked outside in a VIP parking area. He held the door for us, and before long we were weaving through the streets of New York, drinking bottled water and looking at skyscrapers through the sunroof. The driver pulled up outside a marble and glass high-rise hotel.

"Not bad for my first limousine ride." I said.

"Way better than my *only* limousine ride," Kate said. "There were twelve of us crammed in for prom. I had Tricia Davis's puffy taffeta sleeve in my face the entire time. I never told her I got lip gloss on her sleeve. I think her date's dad was the one driving the limo."

"Hopefully this makes up for it," I said.

"Are you okay? You were awfully quiet on the plane." She looked like she was trying to hold back a smile.

"I'm just a little nervous. But Dane said we should just have fun and not worry about anything, so that's what I'm going to try to do."

"Sounds like good advice. And when did Dane give you this pearl of wisdom?" she asked.

"Last night."

"Ah, you squeezed in a little last-minute date?"

"Actually it wasn't so little. It might have been the most perfect date I've ever had."

"Really? Tell me about it."

I told her where we'd gone and what we'd done. I didn't tell her what we'd said. I wasn't ready to share that yet. Right now, that part was just for me.

"You really like him, don't you? Is this going somewhere I should know about?" She was suddenly serious.

"It might be. He's amazing."

I must have sounded a little too dreamy, because Kate smacked my arm and grinned. "I'm really happy for you," she said. "But right now, you've got to focus on *The Today Show* and having fun. Dream about Matt Lauer today, and you can dream about Dane tomorrow."

Having fun turned out to be easy. We checked into the most luxurious room either of us had ever seen. It wasn't large, but it didn't matter. The Chrysler Building was the centerpiece of our view. The bedding was thick and plush with eight pillows on each of the double beds. A huge plasma television hung on the wall, and the bathroom had both a shower and a deep soaking tub.

We walked for a couple of hours around the city, enjoying New York hot dogs and the best papaya smoothie I'd ever tasted. The city was chilly and loud and exciting. We stopped at a souvenir shop where Kate got Izzy a Statue of Liberty bank. Too soon, we headed back to go to bed. *The Today Show* filmed early, and a driver would be picking us up at 5:15 a.m.

"Thank you, *Today Show*, and thank you, Abby," Kate said on the elevator.

At about nine o'clock, Kate called Sam and Izzy. I muted the television and flipped through the channels as she described our exciting day.

"How are they?" I asked when she'd hung up.

"Good. Sam let Izzy rent two princess movies, so she probably thinks I should leave more often," Kate said. "I think I'm going to take advantage of that amazing tub. Do you need anything?"

"No, I'm fine," I said. She'd only been gone for a couple of minutes when I traded the remote for my cell phone. My heart pounded as I dialed Dane's number.

"Hello?"

"Hi," I said.

"Hi," Dane said. He sounded pleased. "I was just wondering if it was too late to call you."

"I guess I beat you to it. I just wanted to say hi."

"How's your day been?" he asked.

"Great. How about yours?"

"It's nice of you to ask, but you're the one in New York, remember?"

I told him about our driver, the hotel, and our hours walking around New York.

"Sounds fun. You're not going to want to come home."

"I am definitely going to want to come home," I said. "Now tell me how your day was."

"It was good. I finished up some cabinets we're doing for a kitchen in Bellevue, not very far from your parents' house."

"Did you stop and say hello?"

Dane laughed. "I'm not sure what they'd think about me dropping in unannounced. They might wonder what's going on."

"You think so?" I asked.

"Unless you've already told them what's going on," he said.

"They know I like you."

"They can probably tell I like you too," he said.

"But I haven't said much else. Should I?"

"Whenever you want."

"Have you said anything to your family?"

"A little. Not everything."

"I guess we have a little secret," I said.

"Where's Kate?" he asked.

"She's in the other room."

"Ah, so that's why you're talking so quietly."

"If I'm not quiet, she'll figure out our secret."

"She probably already knows. They probably all do. We probably don't have a secret at all."

"Are we that obvious?" I asked.

"Probably," he said.

"I wish you were here."

"Me too. I miss you."

I could hear Kate moving around in the bathroom.

"I hear Kate. I should probably go."

"Okay. I'm glad you called."

"Me too."

"I'll see you in the morning."

"You will?" I asked.

"On the show."

"Oh, yeah. Pray I don't make a fool of myself."

"You'll be amazing. Have fun and pay attention so you can tell us every detail about everything."

"I will." We both hesitated, not sure what to say next. I glanced up, and Kate was standing in the doorway watching me. "I'll talk to you later," I said to Dane.

"Good night, Abby."

"Good night." I hung up the phone. Kate eyed me suspiciously.

"What?" I asked.

"How's Dane?" she asked.

"What makes you think that was Dane?"

"Oh, I don't know. Maybe your face. I hope you're not looking like that for Mom and Dad." We laughed, and I threw a pillow at her.

"How was your bath?"

"Don't change the subject."

"I really want to know."

"It was nice. But I don't think it was as good as your phone call."

I rolled my eyes.

"Thanks for coming with me, Kate."

"Thanks for inviting me." She let out a contented sigh as she climbed under the covers. "As much as I'd like to interrogate you about your love life, I think you'd better get a good night's sleep. You have a big day tomorrow."

"You're right. Good night, Kate." I turned off the lamp.

"Good night, Abby." It was quiet for at least a minute. "You're not fooling anyone, you know," she said. I pretended to be asleep.

Twenty

Lemon Chocolate Chip Muffins

2 cups flour
1¼ cups granulated sugar (divided use)
2 tsp. baking powder
2 eggs
¾ cup milk
½ cup butter, melted
2 tsp. grated lemon zest
¼ cup fresh lemon juice
½ cup semisweet chocolate chips

Preheat oven to 375°F. Grease muffin pan or line with paper liners.

In a medium bowl, combine flour, 1 cup sugar, and baking powder. In a large bowl, whisk together eggs, milk, butter, lemon zest, and lemon juice. Stir in flour mixture, mixing just until combined. Fold in the chocolate chips. Do not overmix.

Scoop batter into prepared muffin cups. Sprinkle remaining sugar evenly over tops.

Bake for 20–24 minutes or until muffins are puffed and lightly golden and a skewer inserted into center comes out clean. Let cool in pan on rack for 5 minutes. Remove from pan and let cool completely on rack.

*W*e were dressed and in front of the hotel at 5:15 a.m. Our driver was waiting at the curb, leaning against his car drinking a Styrofoam cup of coffee. A short ride later and we were at the NBC studio. Kate waited in the green room that was really tan and brown, and I met with Melissa to discuss a few last-minute details.

"Great outfit," she said. "That will look perfect on television." I made a mental note to thank Kate for being my personal stylist. After a few minutes, Melissa led me to hair and makeup where I had the full television treatment. By the time they'd made me over, I barely recognized myself. The finished me actually looked worthy of my stylish outfit.

My segment was during the second hour, so I watched the beginning of the show with Kate. An array of pastries and juices filled a table in the corner, but I felt too nervous to eat. When my stomach let out an angry growl, Kate insisted I eat at least part of a muffin. The lemon and chocolate chip muffin tasted so good, I ate the whole thing and then part of a second.

Much too quickly, a producer walked in with a clipboard and an earpiece. "Abby Benson?"

"That's me." I stood up and straightened my skirt.

"Right this way."

Kate grabbed my hand and squeezed it as I left the room. I followed the producer down a short hall and out onto the soundstage where two chairs were sitting. I couldn't help noticing the floor to ceiling windows filled with fans looking in. A middle-aged man made a face that would have made a ten-year-old boy proud, and I tried not to laugh. "Just ignore them," the producer said. She directed me how to sit, and someone fussed for a minute with my hair and powdered my forehead. Then they stepped back and Matt Lauer sat down in the chair opposite me. He was taller and thinner than I'd expected, and I was struck by how much makeup he had on. I'd never have guessed watching it at home. Another surprising thing was how closely we were sitting. We had to carefully place our legs so we wouldn't be awkwardly touching each other. Strange that I'd never noticed that on television.

"Hi, Abby," he said. He leaned forward and shook my hand.

"Hi."

"Don't be nervous. I'm just going to ask you the same questions

Melissa has already asked you. Nothing new. It's not scary."

"Thanks." I squeaked and cleared my throat. I felt a little tongue-tied, and my mind was on overload.

"You look great, by the way." It seemed like he was trying to make me feel more comfortable, but so far it wasn't working. I had trouble catching my breath, and I began to panic. I looked at the window full of people and found the man making faces. He stuck out his tongue. I said a quick, silent prayer that I wouldn't make a fool of myself. Behind me, someone began counting down.

"Have fun and don't worry about a thing," I heard Dane say in my mind.

Matt began speaking. "This week, in our 'Women in the Workplace' segment, we've been bringing you women who have found unusual ways to approach their jobs. Today we're going to introduce you to one woman who decided to try a bold, new strategy not many would have the courage to try. Most people who go into business do so expecting to make money. They set their prices and hope people will buy their product. Abby Benson, the owner of A Piece of Cake in Seattle, Washington, decided not to set prices, but to let the customer do that instead. Was that a good idea? Let's find out."

Beside Matt's chair, hidden from the camera's view, was a small television screen that showed a segment leading up to the interview. We watched the clip that was airing on television. "Meet Abby Benson, owner of A Piece of Cake. Last year, Abby's aunt passed away, leaving Abby everything she needed to fulfill her dream of opening a bakery. With no previous business experience and just her love of baking and decorating wedding cakes, Abby set out on the adventure of a lifetime. She renovated and decorated, and within four months, she was ready to open the doors for business. Her only problem was that she didn't know what to charge. She knew her cakes were beautiful and delicious, but with her lack of experience, she wasn't sure what she could charge.

"At the dinner table with her family, she came up with an unusual plan to let the customer decide what the cake is worth. She knew it was a risk, but she decided to try it." The film clip ended with a still shot of the outside of the bakery, and Matt began to talk to me.

"Abby Benson, good morning."

"Good morning, Matt."

"So how exactly did you come up with this idea that the customer should choose what they want to pay?"

"Well, honestly, I wasn't sure what I should charge. I'd been baking cakes for close to ten years, but that was just for family and friends, so I wasn't sure if I should charge prices that reflected my ten years of cake experience or prices that reflected the fact that I was opening my first shop. I finally decided not to decide. I'd leave that to the customer."

"That had to be a little scary."

"A little. My family thought I'd lost my mind."

"And how has that worked for you?"

"Great for the most part. Some pay more than I would charge, some less. I think overall it's been very fair."

"So tell us about someone who's surprised you and paid more than you would have charged." I told him about the polka dot wedding cake and the kind note that accompanied it.

"But you have been burned before, haven't you?" he asked.

"I have."

"In fact, we have a copy of the note that accompanied that payment." A copy of the note from Mrs. Stratman appeared on the little screen with Mrs. Stratman's name blurred out. Matt read it aloud.

> *Dear Ms. Benson,*
> *The cake was adequate. The service, however, was unacceptable.*
> *We were treated rudely at our initial consultation. We appreciate your method of pricing your cakes, as it makes it possible for us to express our dissatisfaction with your service. We hope this might serve as a lesson to you in the future. Your treatment of the family of the bride and groom is of the utmost importance.*
> *Best wishes in the future.*

"Were you rude?"

"I didn't think so. I tried to direct my questions to the bride and groom, and I guess that offended his mother."

"I see. Let's show the viewers a picture of the cake you delivered to this wedding." A picture of the beautiful five-tiered cake with gold, fondant ribbon swags appeared on the screen. The cake was cropped to minimize the chances that someone would recognize the Stratman's home. "It's a beautiful cake," Matt said.

"Thank you."

"So tell me, Abby, how much did this customer pay?"

"Twenty dollars," I said. Matt gasped a little, and a couple of people off camera snickered.

"Really. How did you react to such an obvious injustice?"

"I called my sister and complained. But she reminded me that I'd decided to do this, so I had to take the good with the bad."

"Did you cash that check?"

"Actually, I have it framed in my office. Of course, I covered up the woman's name and checking account number."

"Do you think you'll continue using this method of pricing?"

"So far I don't see a need to change. The business is growing, and it seems to be working out pretty well. Plus, it's really fun to see what people pay. It's always a surprise, and I love the suspense of it all."

"Well, if I was in the market for a wedding cake, I know where I'd come. Abby, thanks for joining us this morning."

"Thanks for having me, Matt."

The interview ended and we both stood.

"Really amazing. I've never heard of anything like it. Good luck to you." Matt shook my hand before walking over to a couple of couches where Al Roker and Savannah Guthrie were waiting.

"You did great," said Kate as I joined her again in the green room. "You didn't look nervous at all. And you looked gorgeous!"

"Did my voice shake?" I asked.

"Not at all. You were amazing!"

I collapsed onto one of the couches. "It was actually kinda fun. I can't believe I just did that."

A short time later, the driver picked us up in front of the studio. He drove us back to our hotel where we collected our bags, and then he took us on to the airport. We had a couple of hours to kill and we were starving, so we ate burgers at the airport Burger King and watched Headline News as we waited for our flight.

By the time I was buckled into my seat on the plane, the adrenalin had worn off, and I was exhausted. Kate woke me up when the pilot announced we were landing. This time Sam and Izzy were waiting at the bottom of the escalator. Izzy was holding a piece of white poster board that read "Benson/Anderson" in her chubby, little hands. She squirmed out of Sam's arms and hugged Kate.

"I hope you're not too tired," Sam said when we were loaded in the car. "Your Mom and Dad asked us to come over straight from the airport. They want to hear everything about your trip."

"Really? Tonight?" I asked.

"They were worried you might be too tired, but Kate said you wouldn't mind."

Kate looked sheepish. "Oops. I guess I forgot to tell you."

"That's okay. It'll be fun to tell them about it."

When we arrived at their house in Bellevue, I was surprised to see that it wasn't just Dad and Mom. Evan and Nicole were on the couch, and Dane was sitting in a chair on the other side of the room. Our eyes met and held, and his smile was better than those lemon and chocolate chip muffins. I wanted to go straight to him, but I stopped and hugged Dad and Mom before I finally reached Dane. He put his arms out for a hug and I wrapped my arms around his neck and pulled him down for a kiss, not caring who saw. He gave me the comfortable chair and pulled a dining room chair next to it for him.

The questions started immediately. Kate and I hardly had a chance to answer one question before someone asked something else. It was a loud, happy gathering that had been going for nearly two hours when Kate yawned.

"I should probably get her home before she falls asleep right here on the floor," said Sam. He was already holding a sleeping Izzy. "Let me get her in her car seat, and I'll help you get Abby's bags," Sam said to Dane. I wasn't at all disappointed that they'd arranged for Dane to take me home. The party broke up, and soon Dane and I were on our way home.

"Thanks for the ride."

"I'd have picked you up at the airport, but Sam said Izzy was dying to see the big planes, so I decided to surprise you at the house instead."

"It was definitely a surprise. I had no idea you'd be there, or Evan and Nicole."

"Did you think everyone would just want to wait for Sunday? It's not every day that a member of the family is interviewed by Matt Lauer in front of millions." I loved the way he talked about the family, already including himself. "I knew the only way I'd get to see you tonight was if I joined the party. There was no way they were going to let me have you all to myself on your first night back."

"I'm glad you were there." I leaned my head against the back of the seat, too tired to carry on much of a conversation. We held hands all the way home.

In the driveway, Dane left the car running as he came around to open my door. He gathered my bags and put them inside the bedroom door. "You're exhausted, so I'm going to go. Get some sleep, and I'll call you tomorrow." He hugged me tightly. "I'm glad you're home."

"Me too." He kissed me and left.

Twenty-one

Stained Glass on Fondant

fondant covered cake
black royal icing
#2 and #4 icing tip
piping gel in two shades of red and green
small paint brush
simple pattern

With a toothpick, etch the stained glass pattern onto the fondant. Use a light touch. Outline the pattern with black royal icing using the #2 tip. Let sit for an hour or two to dry the royal icing. "Paint" the stained glass with the piping gel using the #4 tip. Use the brush to carefully spread the gel and give a brushed effect. Don't brush after the first ten minutes or so since the gel will begin to firm and will look clumpy.

I expected a spike in business after my appearance on *The Today Show,* and I was right. Much like the days after our local news feature, we were bombarded with calls for appointments and bookings.

April was frazzled at a Tuesday morning staff meeting. She held up a stack of messages. "The days you take booking appointments are completely full, and all of these customers want me to call them back and schedule appointments."

I felt a surge of excitement. It's an intoxicating feeling to have some-thing so completely yours succeed, and A Piece of Cake was succeeding in a way I'd never imagined. I was proud and thrilled, and that stack of messages symbolized how successful the bakery had become. It was scary, but I knew what needed to be done. I hoped April and Lara would agree.

"Here's how I see it." I said. "We either have to turn customers away, or we have to grow with the demand. Opportunities like this are rare, and I don't want to waste it. I want to grow. I've written down a plan, but it won't work without you two, so I really hope you'll both be excited about this." I opened my notebook to my latest list. "The way things are, I don't think we can handle more than eight cakes a week, and even that is too many if we have delivery conflicts."

April raised her hand, and I laughed. "You don't have to raise your hand. I'm not a school teacher."

She put her hand down and spoke. "What would you think about me moving into the kitchen? I'd love to bake and decorate, and maybe we could find another receptionist. I already know how to do some of it, and I could learn the rest."

"I think that's a great idea," Lara said. "With another full-time person in the bakery, we could probably do around a dozen cakes a week."

"Except for deliveries," I said.

"I can start making deliveries," Lara said, "if you think we can afford another van?"

"It's a big investment, but I'm not sure we can afford *not* to have a second van," I said. "Two of us delivering would solve a lot of problems."

It was astonishing to think I was going to hire another person and buy a second van before I'd been in business a year.

"I had two calls Friday afternoon from people wanting to pay in advance," April said. "I told them that isn't how we do it, but one girl said she'd wait and talk to you about it. The other one said she already knows what you're worth and wants to get the payment out of the way. I just thought you'd want to know. They're both coming in later today."

I didn't like the idea of changing our method of payment. Why mess with something that was working so well? It was what had made us unique enough to be on the news. If we changed now, it would feel a little disloyal. Besides, I liked them to taste the cake and listen to their guests rave before they made the payment. To be honest, I liked the suspense and the surprise that came with each payment.

We wrapped up our meeting, and my first call was to LouAnn at the employment agency. Then I called Dane.

"Hey, I was just thinking about you," he said.

"Really?"

"Don't sound so surprised. I think about you all the time." It was hard to remember what I was calling about when he said things like that. "What's new?"

"It's wildly busy. I had more than fifty messages over the weekend." Dane whistled. "I've decided to hire more help. April wants to work in the kitchen, so I'm hiring a new receptionist."

"Wow, it just keeps getting busier," he said. His voice lacked its usual enthusiasm. He was always so supportive and helpful that his tone surprised me. Was he upset? I didn't have time to analyze it because I had an appointment in ten minutes and a cake to finish by five, but a knot had suddenly formed in my stomach. I'd have to sort this out later.

"I'm going to need an appointment so you can fit me in," he said. Whew! He'd cracked a joke. The tightness in my stomach loosened its grip.

"Well, actually, I was wondering if you wanted to do a repeat of minivan shopping and Ivar's."

"Is the Honda giving you problems?" he asked.

"Oh no. The Honda is great. We just have more deliveries than one van can handle. We decided if we get a second one, Lara could help with deliveries that overlap. It would just make everything easier. I was hoping you could help me look for one tonight? I'll even spring for dinner."

"We can fight over the check later. What time did you want to go?"

"I have to deliver a cake at 5, but I'll be back here by 6."

"Then I'll pick you up at 6:30?"

"You're the best. Thanks, Dane. I've got an appointment in just a minute, so I've gotta run. I'll see you tonight."

I was excited. Our last car shopping date had been such an exciting time. It had been our first official date.

"Abby, your appointment is here," April said over the intercom. My thoughts shifted from Dane mode to cake mode.

In the lobby I was greeted by a tinier version of Jada Pinkett Smith (if that's possible) and her best friend. They squealed when they saw me, and for a moment I looked around to see what was so exciting. "Oh, Abby, I'm so, so, so excited that you're going to make my wedding cake." Were they really squealing about me? I couldn't wait to tell Kate. "I told my fiancé I wanted you when I saw you on *The Today Show,* and he said, 'good luck with that,' so I was thrilled, thrilled, thrilled that you had an opening when I called. I'm Angela, by the way."

"I'm Katrina," the friend said.

"It's good to meet you both," I said. "Why don't we sit down right over here and talk about your plans." For the next few minutes, they looked through idea books, and I filled out the order form. "Did you have anything in mind?" I asked.

"Since it's so close to Christmas, we're doing holiday colors, so I'd really like it to be sort of Christmas-y."

"There are several things we can do for Christmas. We could go with something whimsical, like a stack of presents, or we could go with poinsettias or holly. If you want something simple, I could do a clean white, fondant cake with Christmas greens around it and maybe a little holly mixed in."

"What would you have if you were getting married around Christmas?" Angela asked.

"I'd probably go with a cake that looks like stained glass. I could paint poinsettias on the cake. Then when they're outlined in black, it looks like stained glass. It would be really Christmas-y without being as obvious as presents."

"Whoa, girl," Katrina said. "If you don't go with that, I'll have to hunt me down a fiancé before Christmas."

"Don't get any ideas, Kat," Angela said. "Let's do it. I love, love, love the idea of the stained glass."

After a few more questions, she was settled on a four-tier cake with tall layers. It was going to be quite a showstopper. Once the flavors were selected, Angela glanced nervously at Katrina before she started to speak.

"I saw *The Today Show* so I know how you usually do things, but with it being Christmas and all, I'd like to just pay for the cake right now and be done with it. My whole family is heading to New York for the holidays, and they're leaving the day after the wedding—well, except for me and Chet. We'll be going to Costa Rica. But anyway, it's going to be crazy, crazy, crazy and I'd just like to take care of it now. If that's okay."

"I can understand wanting to get everything squared away. But if you haven't seen or tasted the cake, it might be hard for you to decide what the cake is worth."

"Honey, I saw you on that show and I saw what your cakes look like. I have a pretty good idea what it'll be worth."

What could I say? I didn't want to be stubborn or unreasonable. "I guess that would be fine." I reminded myself that this was the way other bakeries handled every payment. That made me feel a little bit better.

"Thank you, thank you, thank you." Angela reached in her purse and pulled out an already sealed envelope. "I'm so excited you're doing my cake. I can't wait to tell people I have the lady from *The Today Show* making my wedding cake."

"I'm happy to do it," I said and slipped the envelope into the order book. She squealed again and hugged me like I was a long-lost friend. When their car was out of sight, I got the envelope out of the order book and opened it. Inside was a check for $2,500. If she'd have still been there, I'd have been the one hugging her.

April came into the kitchen where I was rolling out a sheet of fondant. "Abby," she said quietly. "There's a man here to see you. He doesn't have an appointment, and he won't tell me what it's about, but he said it's important and he really needs to talk to you. I told him you were busy, but he's insistent."

"Thanks, April. Lara, could you finish covering this one for me?" I followed April back out to the showroom. A tall, distinguished man stood across the showroom looking out the front window. He turned when we entered the room.

"How can I help you?" I asked.

"Thank you for seeing me," he said. His tone and manners were formal. He gestured toward the sitting area. "Could I speak to you for a moment?" he asked, gesturing toward the sofa.

"Sure." We sat down and he turned toward me.

"I really must apologize. I didn't realize we'd treated you so unfairly." He shifted uncomfortably in his seat, and it struck me that this was a man unaccustomed to apologizing.

"I'm not sure I know what you're talking about."

"My name is Curtis Stratman. You made my son and daughter-in-law's wedding cake this past summer. I got home from work last week and my wife was extremely upset. She showed me a recording of *The Today Show*. She was embarrassed that the wedding cake from Derreck and Samantha's wedding was displayed along with her note and the story of payment."

"The show was edited so that your name didn't appear anywhere," I said, a little defensively.

"Yes, I know. She's worried people recognized the cake and will know what she did."

I wasn't sure what to say, so I waited. "Miss Benson, my wife handled the entire thing very badly. I'm not sure why she did what she did, but she's terribly embarrassed by the situation. As am I. The cake was wonderful, and I'm ashamed of the way we treated you. I told my wife I'd take care of this, so I want to apologize on behalf of my family and pay you an appropriate amount."

"Oh," I said, momentarily speechless.

Mr. Stratman reached into his inside jacket pocket and pulled out a long business-sized check and handed it to me. It was made out for $2000.

"Thank you, Mr. Stratman. Apology accepted."

"I would like to ask a favor," he said.

"Okay."

"Would you mind if I took the framed check that my wife sent you. I think she would rest easier if she knew no one else would ever see it."

"Of course. I'll go get it." A few minutes later, Mr. Stratman and the framed check were gone. I tried to suppress a smile as I thought of Mr. Stratman handing his wife the framed twenty-dollar check, but it was impossible. I felt completely vindicated.

Twenty-two

Sourdough Bread Bowls

Sourdough Starter

2¼ tsp. active dry yeast
2½ cups lukewarm water
1½ cups bread flour

In a medium bowl, stir the yeast into the lukewarm water. Let the mixture activate (should take about 15 minutes to bubble). Add the bread flour and stir. Cover with a dish towel and let sit for 2–3 days. It's best if you store the starter where the room temperature is warm (80–85 degrees). To keep the starter going, you have to "feed" it: for each 1 cup you take out, replace with ½ cup water and 1 cup flour.

Bread Bowls

3 cups flour
1 Tbsp. salt
1 cup sourdough starter (see above)
½ cup lukewarm water

Combine the flour and salt in a large mixing bowl. Make a well in the center. Give the starter a good stir, because it separates after sitting awhile. Add the starter and the water to the flour and stir until it forms a rough dough. You will probably need to use your hands to work the dough until it comes together into a ball.

Lightly cover a clean work surface with flour and roll the dough in it. Knead until the dough is smooth, elastic, and satiny. Place the dough in a lightly oiled bowl to rise. Cover with a clean dish towel and place in a warm place until the dough has doubled in size (about 2 hours).

Remove the dough from the bowl and punch it down to knock most of the volume out of it. Then knead the bread briefly, just to get it back into a nice ball shape.

Cut the dough in half, then cut each piece in half again. Knead each of the pieces just until they're round again. Form the pieces of dough into ball shapes and tuck any loose edges or seams underneath. Place the dough balls on an ungreased baking sheet as far apart as you can.

Put the baking sheet somewhere warm to let the dough rise a second time until doubled in size (about 1½ hours). Bake at 425°F for 15 minutes and then at 375°F for another 30 minutes. When done, the balls will make a hollow sound when you tap them on the bottom.

Cut a circle in the top and hollow out much of the bread inside to make room for some delicious soup!

*D*ane was waiting in his truck in front of the bakery when I got back from delivering the cake. I pulled into the driveway, and he pulled in behind me. I hate tardiness and here I was, running late. I'd had to wait forty minutes for the florist to arrive so I could arrange the flowers on the cake. Now Dane, always prompt, had been waiting for more than half an hour.

"I'm so sorry. I'm just going to hurry and change. I'll be right out."

"Are you okay?" Dane asked when I came back out in jeans and a white, cotton blouse.

"I'm fine. I just didn't have time to wait on a florist today." I buckled my seat belt and collapsed back onto the seat. Oh, it felt good to sit down. "I'm sorry you had to wait."

"That's okay." He leaned over and kissed my cheek. "Sorry you've had a rough day. Do you want to shop for a van another day and see a movie instead?"

I sighed. "I wish we could. That sounds so nice. But I'd better get the van."

"All right. Car shopping it is."

"You'll never guess who came in today," I said and then told him about Mr. Stratman's visit.

"That took some guts. His wife probably felt like such a fool."

"She must have. I wonder what she'll do with the framed check."

"Probably burn it."

I know it's never a good idea to make comparisons, and I had heard the phrase "you can't go back," but all evening, thoughts of our first minivan date kept creeping into my mind. This time something seemed off. Where Dane had been happy and attentive before, he now seemed quiet and a little distracted. We drove three different vans from two different lots before I settled on another white Honda minivan. It was just like the one I already owned except this one was a year newer and cost a few thousand dollars more.

We drove the new van to the bakery, and now there were two identical white vans in the driveway.

I offered to drive to Ivar's, but Dane said he didn't mind, so we drove to the pier in Dane's truck. Conversation continued to be a little stilted. I told him several stories about the bakery and tried to keep the conversation lively, but when I quit talking, we fell into an uneasy quiet.

We pulled into one of the parking spots across the street from Ivar's. Before Dane could open his door, I put my hand on his arm. "Is everything all right?"

"What do you mean?" he asked.

"I mean, you seem kinda quiet tonight. Is something wrong?"

"I'm fine. You've had a lot going on. I've just been listening." He smiled and patted my hand. "Let's go eat."

We sat near the water on a bench, balancing our bowls of chowder on our laps. The air was warm for October and felt heavy, almost balmy. "My driveway looks a little silly with two identical cars in it," I joked.

"I don't know. I think it looks okay."

"Do you think it would be a good idea to get those magnetic signs to put on the doors? Then when I'm making deliveries, other cars would know I was delivering a cake. Plus it would be good advertising if it had the name and phone number on it."

"Do you think you need more advertising?" Dane asked. "You seem pretty busy."

"That's true, but since I'm hiring another girl, we'll be able to handle a little more business."

"Being *able* to handle it and choosing to handle it are two different things." We looked at each other and Dane shrugged. "I remember when we were here before and your biggest fear was that the bakery would fail. I'm not sure you ever thought about what you'd do if it was really successful."

"I know. It's done better than I could have imagined."

I sensed that Dane had something to say so I waited.

"Is it going the way you want it to?" he asked.

"It's going great. It's growing. I'm hiring new people. And now that Mr. Stratman came and paid me again, the pricing plan has worked out just about perfect." I was rambling, but Dane didn't say anything, so I kept going. "It's hard to believe it's only been six months. Lara and April are amazing. I'm so glad I found them. I think April is going to do great working in the kitchen, and if I can find someone good to replace her, we'll be in good shape. People are paying more and more for the cakes. A girl paid me twenty-five hundred up front today. Didn't even want to wait to see the cake. She said since she saw me on *The Today Show*, she knew right now how much her cake would be worth."

Dane broke his bread bowl into little pieces and threw them out onto the water for the seagulls. For a long time we listened to the birds celebrating their dinner. "Aunt Grace would be shocked," I almost whispered.

"Is it possible to be too successful?" Dane finally asked.

"What do you mean?" The knot in my stomach had returned.

"How big do you actually want it to be?" Dane asked.

"I don't know," I answered.

"What if you outgrow the bakery?"

"Wow, I hadn't thought about that. I doubt that will happen, but if it does, I'll cross that bridge when I get to it."

Looking back, I wonder how I could possibly have been so

thickheaded. Dane was asking valid questions. Questions I'd never stopped long enough to consider. How big did I want the bakery to be? Would I ever move to a larger place if I grew to that point? I had gambled on this pricing idea, and it had turned the bakery into an overnight success. I was proud of myself. Aunt Grace had opened a door for me, but my idea is what had generated so much publicity. I was the one delivering beautiful cakes that people fell in love with and paid huge sums of money for. Part of me was so curious about how far I *could* take it that I didn't pay any attention to that obvious little question of how far I *should* take it. Dane was asking that question, but I was too busy basking in my success to figure out any answers.

Twenty-three

Almond Apple Pandowdy

2 lbs. Granny Smith apples, peeled, cored, and sliced
3 Tbsp. maple syrup
1 Tbsp. lemon juice
¼ cup sugar
1 Tbsp. cornstarch
½ tsp. cinnamon
¼ tsp. nutmeg
¼ tsp. salt
1 (8-oz.) can almond paste
1 (9-inch) refrigerated pie crust

Preheat oven to 400°F. Toss apples with maple syrup and lemon juice in a large bowl. Mix sugar, cornstarch, cinnamon, nutmeg, and salt in a small bowl until well combined. Sprinkle over apples and toss well. Pour into ovenproof skillet.

Between two pieces of waxed paper, roll almond paste into a flat disk that fits the skillet. Place the almond paste over the apples. Lay piecrust over almond paste. Fold in the sides if it's larger than the skillet. Cut three slits through the piecrust and almond paste.

Bake for 30 minutes and remove from oven. Press crust into apples and continue baking for 20 more minutes or until the crust is browned and the filling is bubbling. Cool 20 minutes before serving.

I met Lara at Lincoln Park early in the morning. We were looking for big, healthy leaves we could use as molds on a cake. "I can't believe this really works," she said. She held up a maple leaf that was larger than her hand. "Is this too big?"

"That's a good one. You'll like this cake. It's one of my favorites. We'll roll the fondant out, then lay the leaf on the fondant with the veins down. After that we cut around the leaf and peel it off. We'll have a white leaf that looks just like the original. It's like playing with clay in kindergarten."

"That's so cool. I guess if it works with lace and ribbon, it can work with leaves."

An hour later we were decorating the cake. I'd made a cake similar to this when I was a teenager, baking and decorating my way through *Colette's Cakes*. We glued the white leaves around the cake by brushing a little water on the back of each leaf. They were porcelain-like replicas of the leaves we'd picked that morning. When the cake was covered with leaves, we formed small branches and clumps of grapes as well as a few wild-looking flowers.

"This is the cake I'm having when I get married," Lara said. She slowly circled the cake, taking in each angle. "Pretty but not too girly. Should I place my order now?" she asked.

"Have you set a date?"

"No, but when I do, this is the one."

"This is going to be so much fun," I said to Dane.

"Don't forget a jacket. It might be chilly up there."

"I've got one. And a blanket too."

"Good, I think I've got everything else covered," he said. I stopped at the back of the truck and looked in.

"You found a tandem?"

"That's what you said you wanted. Your wish is my command."

"I've always wanted to ride a tandem bike."

"I had to try four rental shops before I finally found one."

"Thanks for being so determined."

We drove for half an hour to the trailhead of Snoqualmie Valley Trail. Dane told me there was a wonderful biking path that meandered along the river and beautiful old farms. I'd been looking forward to this for weeks.

"We're in for a treat. The leaves are changing, and it isn't too cold," he said.

"It sounds like a perfect day."

And it was. Neither of us had ridden a tandem bike before, and there was definitely a learning curve. We tried to time it just right to get on, but the first time he started out, I wasn't quite ready, and he dragged me a few feet. The second time, I tried sitting on the bike with my feet already on the pedals, but I caused the bike to sway, and it was impossible for Dane to get on. A few tries later, we were laughing so hard, I was nearly crying.

"Okay, we can do this," he said with determination, after the laughter had subsided. "Right foot on the pedal." We both put our right feet on the pedals. "Hands on the handlebars?"

"Yep."

"One, two, three, go." We pedaled in unison, each of us lifting our left leg up to the other pedal at the same time. "Ladies and gentlemen, we have liftoff," he said. Soon we were moving steadily down the trail. "I'd give you a high five, but I think it might ruin our progress."

"I don't think we can stop until we're finished," I said. "We might not be able to get up again."

We rode about ten miles of the trail before turning around. The autumn colors were vivid. In the heavily treed areas, the trail was carpeted with the bright colors. Squirrels scurried across the trail in front of us, and at one point, we even passed two deer grazing about a dozen feet off the trail. We rode through trees and fields and across a couple of bridges. At one point we passed a big, beautiful barn painted a bright aqua. Who paints a barn aqua?

Now I have to make a confession. I enjoyed more than just the views of nature on the bike ride. I also loved my view of Dane. I liked watching his legs work and how he kept us balanced with subtle adjustments.

I liked watching him sit taller and turn to smile at me when one of us said something funny. It felt good to work together, pedaling the bike, in perfect synchronicity. But most of all, I loved how when my legs burned and I didn't know if I was going to be able to finish going up the hill, I could take a little breather and he'd keep going, moving us forward. He was such a good, strong man.

By the time we got back to the truck, it was cooling down fast. Darkness was coming earlier now, and we loaded the bicycle in the truck just as the sun disappeared. Once the exertion of riding the bike was over, it felt cold, and I was thankful for our jackets and the blanket. We drove to North Bend, where we ate hot tomato soup and focaccia bread at George's, a quaint little German bakery and café. It was a lovely place to finish a perfect afternoon. Small tables with white table-cloths were scattered around the small eating area. Stenciling and wood on plaster details made it look like it was straight out of a German fairy tale. The food was served on mismatched antique china and tasted better than anything I'd eaten in ages. We shared a warm piece of pan-dowdy and ice cream that made us sigh with delight.

We held hands as we walked the half block from George's to the truck. Dane opened my door and stepped back to let me in. I looked at him standing there holding the door and I suddenly felt like I would burst. He was good and handsome and strong. He was a gentleman who made me feel comfortable and safe. He was everything I wanted, everything I'd waited for. And he loved me.

"What are you doing?" he asked.

"I'm looking at you," I said. I reached out and grabbed one side of his open jacket and pulled him closer. "You're incredible," I said quietly and kissed him.

"Well, thank you." He wrapped his arms around me. I hugged him tightly inside his coat.

"I mean it," I said. I snuggled into his warmth and kissed him again. "You really are incredible." We stood there for a little while longer. I wanted to stand there forever.

Twenty-four

Peanut Butter Cup Cookie

¾ cup creamy peanut butter
½ cup butter
1¼ cups brown sugar, firmly packed
3 Tbsp. milk
1 Tbsp. vanilla extract
1 large egg
1¾ cups flour
¾ tsp. baking soda
¾ tsp. salt
mini peanut butter cups

Heat oven to 375°F. Combine peanut butter, butter, brown sugar, milk, and vanilla in large bowl. Beat with electric mixer at medium speed until well blended. Add egg. Beat just until blended.

In another bowl, combine flour, baking soda, and salt. Add to creamed mixture at low speed. Mix just until blended. Drop by rounded tablespoonfuls two-inches apart onto greased baking sheet. Press a mini peanut butter cup into the center of the cookie.

Bake for 7–8 minutes or until set and just beginning to brown. Cool for 2 minutes on baking sheet before removing to cooling racks to finish cooling.

*bby," Kelly said over the phone, "you've got a call on line two. They only want to speak to you."

"Thanks, Kelly, I'll take it at my desk." I wiped my hands on my apron and picked up the phone in my office. Kelly had been working for just two weeks, and already I didn't know how we'd survived without her. She was older than the rest of us—probably close to forty. She was married with a son in high school. LeeAnn had sent three women over to interview—a teenager just out of high school, a twenty-something, and then Kelly. About two questions into the interview, I knew she was the one I wanted. She was extremely organized and gave a mature credibility that I liked. April was working out well in the kitchen, and even though we were extremely busy, things were running pretty smoothly.

"Hello, this is Abby," I said.

"I can't believe I'm actually talking to you. This is McKenzie Merriweather."

"Excuse me?" I said. I must have heard her wrong.

"This is McKenzie Merriweather." She laughed. "I promise this isn't a prank phone call. It really is me."

"Hi," I said, and I think my voice cracked a little. "What can I do for you?" I felt a little intimidated. McKenzie Merriweather was one of those people who somehow got blessed with it all—a great voice, supermodel good looks, and the right connections. She was the daughter of Lester Merriweather, the actor, but she chose not to follow the family business, exactly, and instead went into music. Not the teenybopper bubble gum variety but great music that she wrote herself. She had been nominated for three Grammys but had never won. And now I was talking to her on the phone.

"I'm getting married on January 22, and I wanted to talk to you about our wedding cake. I saw you on *The Today Show* and loved your cakes."

"Oh. Thank you."

"I'm actually working with a wedding consultant, but I really wanted to talk to you myself."

"So are you getting married in the Seattle area?" I asked. I was proud of myself. I had found my voice and was doing a pretty good job at sounding professional.

"No, I'm getting married at a vineyard in Napa Valley. I talked to my wedding consultant, and she can arrange for you to do the cake in California. She can work out the details with you, but she can arrange to get you a kitchen to work in, and of course we'll fly you and an assistant down here to do the cake. We'll take care of your hotel and anything else you'll need. I have something in mind, and I know you're the right one for the job. Please say you'll do it. I really have my heart set on it."

"Let me check my schedule and make sure I have that day available."

"Sure. I'll just wait." I put McKenzie Merriweather on hold and punched Kelly's number.

"Kelly, do we have any bookings yet for January 22?" I heard her typing into the high-tech computer scheduling system that had recently replaced our old scheduling binder.

"You don't have anything yet."

"What day of the week is that?" I asked.

"It's a Saturday."

"Do we have anything else that week?"

"We have Bailey Ellis on Tuesday, Casey Ling on Thursday, and Allison Mishling on Friday."

"Would you please block out the rest of that week? I'll give you the details later."

"Done," she said.

I punched Mckenzie Merriweather's line. "It looks like I'm available," I said.

"Oh, that's wonderful. I'm going to send Lucinda up to finalize the details. Can you meet with her this weekend?"

"Actually, I'm doing the bridal fair this weekend, so I won't be in the bakery."

"How about next week?"

"That should be fine," I said. "Just have her call Kelly and set up the appointment."

"Excellent! I'm so glad you're going to do this. I have some pictures I've drawn that I'll send up with Lucinda. The two of you can work out all the details. Thank you, Abby."

"You're welcome." I felt ridiculous that McKenzie Merriweather was acting like I was doing her a favor. Doing the wedding cake for someone like her would be a major feather in my cap. Maybe the cake would be featured in a magazine. Imagine what that would do for business.

On top of the bridal fair that lasted all day Friday and Saturday as well as Sunday afternoon, we had two cakes during the week. There was so much to do that after making three of the five dummy cakes I'd planned for the fair, I opted out of the last two and picked two from the showroom to take with me. I was really happy with the way my booth looked. I brought a laptop loaded with my schedule and more photos of cakes so I could handle bookings on the spot. I hated that the bridal fair was also on Sunday, but at least it was in the afternoon so I was able to go to sacrament meeting before running over to the trade center.

Lara, with April's help, finished and delivered the cake for Saturday. I was a little disappointed that I couldn't do it. They delivered it to a yacht moored in Puget Sound. The wedding and reception were taking place out on the water. It sounded beautiful, and I wished I could have seen it. The compensation was that during the bridal fair, I booked twenty-six weddings. Twenty-six weddings in only two and a half days! My head was spinning.

On Saturday evening, the bridal fair sponsored a fashion show. There were dozens of wedding gowns, bridesmaid dresses, and tuxedos. Many of the vendors left their booths with cards and brochures displayed and went to watch the fashion show. I had planned to attend but was so tired, I decided to sit in my booth and relax instead. I closed my eyes and must have dozed for a moment because I was awakened by a kiss on the cheek. I opened my eyes to see Dane standing in front of me.

"What are you doing here?" I was so happy to see him.

"I have to see my girl sometime," he said. I made a mental note of the "my girl" reference and noticed that my heart was beating faster.

"You didn't pay to get in did you?"

"Gotta do what I gotta do."

"Oh, I wish I'd have known you were coming. I've got two assistant passes. I could have given you one of them."

"It's not a big deal. I just wanted to see you. I haven't seen you all week."

"I know. Sorry. How have you been?"

"Good. We're working on a kitchen remodel in Renton. It's a big one, and they want to have her parents' fiftieth wedding anniversary there, so we've been putting in some long hours to get it finished."

"Another family project with a family deadline. You like those, don't you?"

"Some of them better than others." The mischievous twinkle in Dane's eye made me catch my breath. I had to do a better job of managing my time. How could I let an entire week go by without seeing him?

"Man, I've missed you," I said. I was surprised to hear myself say the words out loud.

"I've missed you too. Let's take a little walk. I could use a drink of water, and it probably wouldn't hurt you to get out of this booth for a few minutes." We walked out into the convention center lobby and found a concessions area where we purchased two bottled waters and a Reese's peanut butter cup cookie. We sat on a bench by the floor-to-ceiling windows that looked out over the city.

Dane made circles with his thumb on my hand and then pulled my hand up and kissed it. "So, my uncle in Portland just bought an old craftsman home that he wants to restore."

"I didn't know he was a builder."

"He's not. He's a banker. He just likes what I've done with mine, so when he found a good deal on one down there, he snatched it up. He called this week to see if I wanted to come down there for a few months and be the general contractor for the restoration."

"Oh," I said. I felt like the wind was knocked out of me. "How long would you be gone?"

"If I moved down there and took on the job, I'd be gone at least two or three months."

I took a deep breath and blew it out slowly. "Do you want to do it?"

"That's just it. I don't think I do. I told him I'd be glad to come down and work with whoever he finds, maybe spend a few days every couple of weeks, but I told him this wasn't really a good time for me to leave." I started breathing again. I looked at Dane and found that he was watching me intently. "Did I tell him the right thing?" he asked.

What did that even mean? Was he asking me if he should go? Of course I didn't want him to go. Was he hinting at something bigger? It seemed like he was.

"Yeah, I think you did," I said. I hugged his arm and leaned my head on his shoulder. He kissed my hair.

"Good. I was hoping so."

I wasn't sure what had just happened. I wanted to process this whole conversation and figure out what it meant. I wanted to leave with him right now. The last thing I wanted to do was go back into the conference center and help other girls plan their weddings.

"Hey. I haven't told you yet. Guess whose wedding cake I'm making in January?"

"Whose?"

"You won't believe it. I'm doing McKenzie Merriweather's wedding cake."

"Really? Is she from up here?" he asked.

"That's exactly what I wondered. She's getting married at a vineyard in Napa Valley, and they're going to fly me down there to make the cake. She wanted *me*. Can you believe it? She actually called me on the phone herself. Her wedding consultant is going to come up and finalize the order next week. I can't even believe it. She said she saw me on *The Today Show* and had her heart set on me making the cake."

"What are you going to charge her? I mean, what do you think she's going to pay?"

"I don't know, but who cares? They're flying me down there, and I get to make the wedding cake for a huge celebrity. Can you imagine? Maybe they'll show the cake in *People Magazine* or something. Talk about great publicity."

"That's pretty cool," Dane said. "I like a couple of her songs. You'll have to tell me if she's as pretty in person as she looks on TV."

"Are you trying to make me jealous?" I asked.

"Absolutely not," he said. "I'd choose you any day." He leaned over and kissed me. This half an hour had to be one of the best ever. I wanted Dane to take me home. My legs felt like lead, and a little headache had been building behind my eyes all day long, a reminder that I really needed some sleep.

And Dane had just told me he'd choose me over McKenzie

Merriweather, and he'd told his uncle this wasn't a good time for him to go to Oregon. There was so much to daydream about. I sighed. "I'd better get back over to the booth," I said. "I wish we could just leave together right now."

"So do I." We walked back to my booth. The fashion show must have ended because the aisles were filling up with people and vendors were hurrying back to their booths. Soon I was surrounded by people with questions. Dane caught my eye and pointed at himself and then at the exit. He smiled and mouthed "good-bye," and he was gone. I felt strangely sad as I watched him walk away.

Lucinda Schmidt arrived in a cab carrying only a briefcase. The only purpose of her trip was to meet with me. She came directly from the airport, and when we were finished, the driver took her back to catch the next flight. Lucinda wasn't anything like the breezy, pretty California party planners I'd seen on television and in movies. She was severely dressed in a gray, tailored suit and had short, spiky, red hair— the kind of red that almost looks burgundy and doesn't appear any-where in nature. She was cordial, but all business.

"How are you, Ms. Benson?" she asked, shaking my hand with a weak I-don't-really-want-to-touch-your-hand handshake.

"I'm fine, thank you. How was your flight?"

"Excellent. Shall we get started?" She sat in one of the straight-backed chairs and opened her briefcase. I sat down as she pulled out a few sketches of McKenzie's idea for her cake. Or should I say, cakes. She had sketched an enormous cake that would be in the center of the reception. At each table was a single cake—about eight inches tall— that looked like a layer of the center cake. These would be the table centerpieces. It would be impressive. I was glad I'd had Kelly block out the week. I was going to have to take Lara or April with me. One person wouldn't be able to pull off all these cakes in a week.

I was impressed. McKenzie Merriweather was an artist. The top picture was of the main cake—a five-tiered showpiece. The tiers were taller than usual—about ten inches per tier—giving it impressive height. The entire cake was white with tiny, black, lace-like piping cov-ering the entire cake. A black fondant ribbon about two inches wide circled the bottom of each tier. In the back, all five ribbons were tied with bows. Another beautiful detail on the back was a row of tiny, black, pearl buttons, fashioned from fondant that went from the top of the cake to the bottom, giving the cake the look of the back of a beautiful dress. It really was stunning. "I've reserved a kitchen at the Napa Valley Culinary Institute. You'll have it the entire week. Do you think that will give you sufficient time?"

"I think so," I said. I remembered a special I'd seen on the Food Network about the Napa Valley Culinary Institute. Who would ever have thought I'd someday be baking there? For McKenzie Merriweather!

"We'll book you and an assistant a flight, a rental car, and a hotel. I thought we'd book your flight for Sunday so you'll have as much time there as possible."

"That should be fine." I was happy to let Lucinda manage all these details. She seemed to know what she was doing far better than I did.

"They have good equipment there," she said. "Your contact person will be Emil Graffard. He can go over the equipment with you to be sure you have everything you need. I've attached his card with all the information you should need. He's also prepared to purchase your ingredients if you decide you'd like him to do that."

"Oh, that's okay. I actually prefer to do that myself. I can do that first thing Monday morning."

"I thought you might prefer that, but just know he's available should you need him."

A short time later, we had a deposit and a signed contract, and Lucinda was on her way back to the airport.

Twenty-five

Raspberry Cream Filling

1 (about 10.5-oz.) pkg. frozen raspberries
1 cup sugar
4 oz. water
2½ tsp. powdered, unflavored gelatin
2 cups heavy cream

Place frozen raspberries, sugar, and water in a medium saucepan and bring to a boil. Allow the liquid to cook down and thicken up a bit. (If you don't want raspberry pieces in your filling, you can strain it at this point.)

Place ¼ cup purée and gelatin in a heatproof measuring cup and let it sit over a pan of simmering water for 5 minutes, stirring until the gelatin is dissolved. Remove gelatin mixture from heat and stir in with the rest of the purée. Allow the purée to come down to room temperature.

Beat the heavy cream in a mixer bowl until it forms soft peaks. Add the purée mixture and beat until soft peaks form.

You can fill your cakes at this point or chill the mixture. It will chill up pretty firm, like a mousse.

*H*appy birthday, dear Dane. Happy birthday to you!" We finished the song and everyone clapped as Dane blew out the candles on the raspberry cream–filled lemon cake I'd made for his birthday.

"What did you wish for, Uncle Dane?" Ruby asked.

"I can't tell or it won't come true." Dane tugged on her pigtail, and she giggled.

"I'll bet I know what he wished for," Blake said.

"Blake, that's enough," Mrs. Reynolds said. Her voice was stern, but she had a smile on her face.

"This cake is delicious," Mr. Reynolds said. "Lemon's not usually my favorite, but after tasting this, I might have to rethink that."

"I'm glad you like it," I said.

"Abby, it sounds like you've been a busy girl," Mrs. Reynolds said.

"I sure have. It's almost overwhelming," I said. "I thought it would take years to get to this point. This is much faster than I expected."

"I guess appearances on the news and *The Today Show* help," Sarah said.

"And celebrities ordering from you," said Mrs. Reynolds. "Did you hear she's doing the wedding cake for some singer?" she asked Sarah.

"Really? Who?" Sarah asked.

"McKenzie Merriweather." I suddenly felt self-conscious, like I was a name-dropper.

"You're kidding. How did that happen?"

I'd just put a bite of cake in my mouth, so Dane answered. "McKenzie Merriweather saw Abby on *The Today Show* and decided right on the spot that she wanted Abby to do her cake. She sent her wedding planner up here last week to finalize everything."

"Wow." Sarah was impressed.

"They're flying Abby down to Napa Valley to do the cake in January."

"That's so cool," Sarah said.

"I was pretty shocked by the whole thing," I said.

"Pretty soon you're going to have to find yourself a bigger space," Mr. Reynolds said.

"I don't think so. The shop is big enough to support even more than I'm doing now, so I think I'll be fine there. It helps that I only do wedding cakes and not bread or donuts. Well, I guess I do make an occasional birthday cake." I looked at Dane and smiled, only to find that he wasn't looking at me. He was looking at his mom who was exchanging looks with Mr. Reynolds. I continued looking around the room. Sarah and Blake were looking at each other. In fact, everyone seemed to be looking at each other, but no one would make eye contact with me. A sudden awkwardness filled the air. What had I missed? I looked back at Dane, who was now looking down at his cake. My eyes bored into him, but he didn't look at me.

What was going on? Mrs. Reynolds took a deep breath. I, on the other hand, felt like something was squeezing the air out of my lungs.

"Did I just miss something?" I asked. My voice felt weak, and I did my best to keep it steady.

"I just wonder how such a busy shop is going to fit in with having a family," Dane's mother said. She spoke in a cheerful tone, but it didn't feel genuine.

"I'm sure I'll work it out," I said. I glanced at Dane, who continued to stare at his plate. "I guess I'll cross that bridge when I get there." I blinked hard against the hot sting of tears. I would not cry in front of them. I felt attacked but couldn't think what I'd done wrong. Why wouldn't Dane look at me? Why wasn't he sticking up for me? He just sat there moving a crumb of cake around on his plate.

"I'm sure you will," Mr. Reynolds said. The kindness in his tone made me want to hug him. The room was quiet for a moment before Mr. Reynolds continued. "Blake, you and Dane need to drive by that duplex on Adelaide and see if you think it's worth investing in. I think we could get it for a lot less than they're asking, and once we remodel it, we can either sell it or rent it out. I think it's a good piece of property."

"Sure, Dad," Blake said. "We can go see it tomorrow."

Sarah stood and gathered up empty plates.

"I'll help you with that," I said. I took Dane's plate from his hands without looking at his face and followed Sarah into the kitchen.

"Sorry about that," Sarah said. "She's just worried about Dane, and she's never been very good at waiting things out. She always wants to jump in and fix the problem."

I rinsed off the dishes and stacked them on the counter. "I'm not sure I understand what needs to be fixed."

"She knows Dane's fallen for you. Pretty hard."

"So?"

"So Dane has always wanted lots of kids. That's why he broke up with the last girl he was serious about. She didn't really want kids. She said she was willing to have one or two for him, but it wasn't important to her at all."

"I want kids. I've always wanted kids."

"But his mom is worried your bakery will make it hard to have a family."

"Maybe Dane should talk to me about it," I said. I didn't like this conversation. We weren't engaged. In fact, Dane hadn't ever mentioned marriage at all. Was I supposed to hold back the bakery just in case Dane decided he wanted to marry me? That didn't seem fair.

"Of course he should talk to you," Sarah said. "But guys aren't always brave when it comes to hard discussions with a girl they've fallen in love with. I wouldn't worry about it. And don't be mad at his mom. She's just looking out for her son."

That comment annoyed me. She was looking out for him—like I was something he needed to be protected from.

We stayed another hour or so, but the conversation went on around me. I could feel my frustration and anger building. I wanted to leave. I wanted to talk to Dane about what had just happened. But instead we sat and listened to Blake and Mr. Reynolds talk about an apartment complex they'd sold two years ago and how glad they were they'd sold it when they did. Dane didn't say much. It was like there was a wall of awkwardness built around us. I think we only stayed because Dane didn't want to have to face me. When Blake and Sarah gathered their kids to go, we said good-bye. Mrs. Reynolds didn't hug me good-bye like she usually did. She didn't hug Dane either. I noticed and wondered if it meant something.

I waited until we'd backed out of the driveway before I spoke. "What was that all about?" I asked.

"It was no big deal," he said.

"No big deal? Your mom completely disapproves of me. In fact, I feel like the whole family does, but your mom is the only one with guts enough to say something. Did you see everyone looking at each other, trying to decide if they should pounce on me or not?"

"I think you're overreacting a little."

"Do you really? And you just sat there. You didn't say a word. You didn't stick up for me or change the subject or smile at me. Nothing.

You wouldn't even look at me. You just stared at your plate."

"I guess I wanted to see what your answer would be."

"If you want an answer to something, ask *me* a question. What do you want to know? Come on. Ask me."

"Abby, let's talk about this some other time."

"No, let's talk now. I just sat there being judged by your entire family for more than an hour. Let's get you the answers you want but haven't asked me for. You've never asked me what I want to do with the bakery after I get married or how many kids I want to have or anything. I guess you're just waiting for your mom to ask for you. And Jessica." My voice was rising. I wanted to stay calm, but I felt like I had no control over my tone of voice. "I'm constantly being compared to Jessica, the tall blonde beauty who I learned tonight didn't really want kids. I don't want to be compared to Jessica. I don't compare you to any of the guys I used to date. And neither does my family."

"Abby, calm down." Dane reached for my hand. I pulled it away and turned toward the window. The tears I'd been fighting off for more than an hour came in a torrent. Once they started, I couldn't stop them. I tried to wipe them away without Dane seeing, but they wouldn't stop.

I hadn't realized where we were going until Dane pulled into a parking lot facing Puget Sound. He turned off the car, and we sat in silence for a long time. Thoughts tumbled over themselves in my mind. I couldn't believe how hurt I felt—like a piñata pummeled at a party of sixth-grade boys. We'd never talked about any of these things. What was I supposed to think? I'd just thought he was moving slow. I hadn't realized that he'd been holding off because he thought I was too caught up in my career.

These thoughts went through my mind over and over as I allowed my hurt pride to overtake reason. What had he said to his family? I wasn't some career woman who'd tossed marriage and family aside. The entire bakery had been something I'd never planned on, and now I was being misjudged because of its success. Of course I wanted a family. I'd had names picked out for ten years, for crying out loud. Did Dane have any names picked out?

"Abby . . ." His pleading voice finally broke the silence. It was as if the sound of his voice flipped a switch inside me. Instantly I found my voice, and when I started talking, I couldn't stop.

"What is wrong with your mom?" I said. "This isn't the first time I've felt like she was attacking me about my bakery. Is she afraid her little boy can't take care of himself?" As I heard the words come out of my mouth, I was shocked at how hateful I sounded. But I continued. "Do you always let her do *your* dirty work?"

"Abby, stop it. Can we have a real talk here without fighting or saying things we'll regret?"

"I don't know, Dane. Can we? Maybe we're not capable of having a real talk. Maybe we're fine as long as everything is just fun and easy. Maybe when it comes to a *real* conversation about *real* things, it just isn't possible for us. I know more about Jessica from your family than I do from you. I know more about how you feel about kids from your family than I do from you. In fact, I don't know much about you, do I?"

"You do too. This is crazy. Just calm down and let's talk. Please."

"I'm calm," I said, purposely lowering my voice and keeping it steady and free of emotion. "If you want to talk, please, talk." I knew I wasn't creating a good environment for sharing feelings, but my feelings were hurt, and I felt like the most important part of who I was had been attacked. I felt justified in being angry.

Dane was quiet and the seconds ticked by.

"I said talk. I'm waiting for some incredible insight into the Dane I don't know. Go ahead. Talk." My voice was cold and steely.

Dane took a deep breath and began. I kept my hard gaze focused on the water in front of us. I knew I was making it hard for him, but I felt like he deserved it. It had been hard for me sit in his living room, the center of unwelcome attention. He hadn't made it easier for me, so I'd let him struggle through this.

"Abby, all my life I've wanted a happy family—a wife I adore and lots of kids. I've tried to find a girl who wants the same things as me. I've really tried. But somehow I keep getting it wrong. I'm twenty-seven years old today. That may not sound that old, but Blake is less than two years older than me and he's going to have his third kid in six months."

I hadn't even realized Sarah was pregnant. So much for keeping me up on the family news.

"I'm ready to move ahead and take the next step in my life," he said.

This was so wrong. Here was Dane, saying all the things I'd dreamed of him saying, but he was doing it when my reason and judgment were clouded by hurt. Part of me wanted to reach over and hug him and tell him I was sorry and I loved him and I wanted those things too. I wanted to tell him that all he had to do was ask me and I'd be there, ready to take the next step with him.

Part of me wanted to say those things, but I let my anger and my hurt feelings get in the way. I sat there with my arms folded tightly, looking straight ahead.

Dane kept trying. "I love you, Abby. I knew you were different almost from the moment we met. You're not like the other girls I've dated. You're such a 'mom' type that I knew you'd be a great mother." Dane couldn't have given me a compliment I'd have loved more. Why did he have to say such a perfect thing in the middle of a fight? I almost melted. "But now you're so busy. Your bakery is taking more and more of your time, and the bigger it gets the less time I see for a family, and I'm not sure where you want the bakery to go. I'm not sure where you want *us* to go. I feel like I'm losing you to the bakery, and then I feel guilty because I should be happy that you've done so well. I know it sounds selfish, but things aren't headed in the direction I pictured them going."

"Dane, are you serious? You think that because you smiled at me and kissed me that I should just hold off on the bakery, hoping maybe those things would lead to marriage and children? Have you ever, *ever*, said that you want to marry me or that you want to have kids with me? No. You haven't. I'm supposed to rein in the bakery just in case you decide to ask me to marry you."

"Okay, so it doesn't make sense. I didn't say I'm a great communicator. I just know how I've been feeling, and I hoped you were feeling the same way. I want to marry you, but every time I turn around, something is happening with the bakery. It's getting bigger and bigger, and it's filling up your life, and I feel like what I was hoping for is getting squeezed out."

Dane had just said he wanted to marry me. What was wrong with him? Why did he have to tell me that now when I was so hurt and angry? And why couldn't I stop myself from doing damage?

"Too bad you've never told me what you hope for. Too bad you've never told me what you really want."

"I know, Abby. But try to see how it looks to me. You're on TV.

The bakery gets bigger. Then you're on TV again. You're making thousands of dollars on a single cake. You're getting busier and busier. You're hiring new people. And now you're flying to California to make cakes for celebrities."

"For *one* celebrity," I emphasized the singular.

"And you're always talking about the free advertising, the good publicity. Do you need any more of that? That seems like something you'd want if you want the bakery to grow bigger and bigger. What am I supposed to think?"

"Ask me if you want to know something. You know, Dane, if you asked me, I could tell you. I want kids. I've had names picked out for years. I want to be a mom. I want to be married. I want to be a good wife and a good mother. Of course I want those things. There. Now you know. Too bad you couldn't have just asked me what I think instead of avoiding the subject or trying to find out what I think by turning your family loose on me." I let out a long sigh. I suddenly felt tired. "Could you please take me home?"

"I want . . ."

"Please, Dane. Just take me home." I turned to the window as the hot tears burned my cheeks.

Dane let out a heavy sigh and sat there quietly. He reached over and rubbed my back, but I didn't return his touch. Finally he turned on the car, and we drove home without talking. When he pulled into the driveway, I opened the door almost before the car had come to a stop. I slammed it and walked toward the house, without turning to look at him.

I wanted him to follow me. I wanted him to say "Now that we know what we both want, let's get married." I walked in the house, threw myself on the bed, and waited. I wanted to hear his knock on the door. I listened intently, focused on the sound of his engine in the driveway. I held my breath and listened. His car continued to idle for several minutes, and I was sure he was going to come to the door. *Come on, Dane. Turn the car off. Come in. Please come in.* I wiped my tears away so I'd look more presentable when he came to the door. I thought about what I'd say, how I'd throw my arms around him and tell him how much I loved him. I wanted to tell him he was the most wonderful man I'd ever dated and that I wanted to spend the rest of my life with him.

But after ten minutes, I heard him put the car in gear, and then the sound of the engine faded away. And I cried again. I didn't even change for bed or brush my teeth. I just cried myself to sleep.

How to Ruin a Birthday

One birthday boy
One misunderstood girl
One overly concerned mother

Mix together for an afternoon. Separate boy and girl from mother. Stir in hurt feelings, misunderstandings, and harsh and hasty words. Pour in plenty of tears and let simmer. If love and forgiveness try to rise to the surface, beat them back down with defensiveness. Separate boy and girl and let each marinate in their own pain.

*A*bby, you look awful. Are you sick?" April asked when I walked into the showroom.

"I'm fine," I said. "I just didn't sleep very well last night." I knew I looked terrible. Twenty minutes with a package of frozen peas on my eyes had done nothing to reduce the puffy bags that a night of crying had caused. Thankfully, the conversation only had to be repeated one more time since Lara and Kelly arrived at the same time. I don't think any of them believed I was fine, but we all got to work, finishing the two cakes we would to deliver that day.

I woodenly finished the topsy-turvy cake I'd been so excited to do. I cut out the bright yellow diamonds of fondant that would make the harlequin pattern, lightly brushed water on the back, and lined them up on the lopsided pale yellow cake. Lara talked about a movie she'd seen the night before with her boyfriend. I gave little responses where they were expected, but I couldn't even remember the name of the movie a couple of minutes later. The easy conversation that usually filled the kitchen was impossible, and after a while we worked in silence. I was glad. I wanted quiet so I could think. I knew I'd made a mess of my life last night. I worried that the damage was irreparable. I felt an ache in my heart, and I had to get away.

I felt Lara and April's eyes on me as I stepped into my office and closed the door. I leaned against the closed door and cried again. I slid to the floor and sat there for several minutes, crying into the sleeve of my shirt. Finally, I returned to the kitchen to finish the cake, my eyes red and stinging.

"I love it," Lara said when I stood back to look at the finished cake. It was a fun and eye-catching cake, but I couldn't muster any enthusiasm about it. I just didn't care.

"Do you two want to make this delivery?" I asked. They looked at each other, surprised. I'd only missed a delivery when two cakes had been scheduled for the same time and once during the bridal fair. This request was a sure sign I was not okay. "This one's going to The Boathouse, and it needs to be there at three. I can have the other one ready when you get back."

"Abby, are you sure you're okay?" Lara asked.

"I'm sure. The second one goes to the Presbyterian church out on Old Man's Loop, but it doesn't have to be there until six."

"If you're sure," Lara said.

"I'm sure." I got the keys and the camera out of the office. Lara carried the cake to the back of the car while April held the umbrella over the cake to protect it from a light drizzle. "Do you need anything before we go?" April asked.

"I'm good. Thanks, you guys. Don't forget to get pictures."

I was glad to be alone with my thoughts as I rolled ivory coloring into a small piece of fondant. I imagined calling Dane and apologizing. I pictured him hugging me and telling me it would be okay. At that point, he would ask me to marry him, and we'd put this entire thing behind us.

I rolled the piece of fondant out like a rope and rolled a piece of grosgrain ribbon into it, transferring the texture from the ribbon to the fondant. Then I trimmed the sides. It felt good to have something to keep my hands busy while my mind thought of Dane. I attached the ribbon to the side of the cake. I repeated the process for each tier. In my mind I relived last night's conversation. It was ugly, and I felt ashamed. I wanted to start it over. I couldn't believe some of the things I'd said. What had come over me? The reactions of Dane and his family to my bakery were natural and understandable. It *was* getting big and busy and time-consuming. Even life-consuming. Yet I had struck back at him like he was wrong. I knew I needed to make things right. I had to. I needed to apologize.

I stepped back to look at the cake. It was simple and beautiful—just the way I wanted my life to be. I walked into my office and sat at my desk. I was feeling a little better. Dane was supposed to come to dinner at my family's tomorrow. After the things I'd said last night, I knew that would be uncomfortable for him. I'd let my hurt feelings be an excuse to be unkind.

In my heart I knew what Dane wanted and where things were going. I'd known that eventually he'd get around to saying those things and asking those questions. Dane and I were going to end up together. I'd felt that for months now. Dane was the best man I'd ever dated. I cried new tears now. Instead of crying over my own hurt feelings, I thought about how I'd ruined his birthday. I would apologize. But I wanted to do it in person, and I didn't want to do it on the way to Sunday dinner. He probably didn't want to come anyway under the circumstances. I picked up the phone and dialed his home number, knowing I'd get his machine at this time of day.

"This is Dane. I'm not home right now. Leave your name and number and I'll call you as soon as I can." Just hearing his voice lifted my spirits a little. I longed to talk to him, but I didn't want to talk on the phone until I'd apologized.

"Hi Dane. This is Abby. I just wanted to let you know that you don't have to come to Sunday dinner with me tomorrow. I'm sure after last night it would be awkward, so don't worry about it. Okay. I'll talk to you soon. Um, bye." I felt good letting him off the hook, like I was making up a little bit for last night by sparing him the awkwardness.

I'd see him soon, and I'd tell him how sorry I was for overreacting and how much I loved him. We'd talk about what we want and we'd have a real conversation. Then we'd move ahead with the rest of our lives. I smiled as I thought about how nice it would be to have our first big fight behind us.

I felt much better when April and Lara got back and even cracked a couple of jokes with them. I could tell they were relieved. I sent Lara home to get ready for a concert, and April went with me to deliver the grosgrain ribbon cake.

"Where's Dane?" Mom asked when I walked into the house Sunday afternoon.

"He couldn't come today after all."

"Everything okay?" She sounded suspicious.

"Everything's fine, Mom." I grabbed a cherry tomato off the salad and plopped it into my mouth.

"What's new at the bakery?" Evan asked as we began dishing up the roasted chicken and rice.

"It's busy," I said.

"Is it too busy?" Dad asked. The concern in his voice made me realize that Dane and his family weren't the only ones with concerns about the bakery taking over my life.

"I don't know about too busy. I mean, I can decide how busy I want to be. I can always turn down bookings, you know." I listened to my voice sounding too defensive again and decided this was a good time to turn the conversation another direction. "I'm wondering what you think about something though. Some people want to pay up front, instead of waiting until they get their cake. It makes everything different."

"Is that a bad thing?" Dad asked.

"I don't know if it's bad. It's just different. How can they know what the cake is worth, if it hasn't even been delivered yet. They haven't seen the finished product or tasted it or anything."

"That's true, but maybe they've decided the cake is worth what it takes to get *you*. Your stock has gone up considerably. I'm not sure that should be a problem though." Everyone was listening, but so far no one but Dad had said anything.

"I guess it isn't really a problem," I said. "I'm going to deliver a great cake either way. I just like the way things have been going, and I'm not sure I want to change it. It's fun to get paid later. I like the suspense or the delayed gratification, maybe. And it feels like a present when it comes later."

"What do they say when you explain how your pricing works?" Sam asked.

"I almost never have to explain anymore. Most of the people who are calling already know how I price the cakes and they just want to be sure they get to book with us. Kelly said one woman called and said some ridiculous thing like 'I'll pay four thousand dollars to book you on such and such a date.' It seems crazy."

"It doesn't to me," said Sam. "When you started out, you had to show them the finished product in order for them to decide what it was worth. Now they've seen your finished products on the local news and *The Today Show*. They know what the cake will be like. They're not paying what the cake is worth anymore. They're paying what they think you're worth."

"I think it's great," said Dad. "You've made quite a name for yourself."

"I don't know. It just feels like . . ." It was hard to explain that the way most businesses charged for their services didn't feel right to me.

"Abby, you don't have to feel guilty that people are paying you so much," Kate said.

I turned and stared at her. Did she know me better than I knew myself? I hadn't been able to figure out why I was bothered, but when she said it, I recognized it. I felt fine about customers paying a large sum for a cake, but when they paid in advance, it was like they were paying that huge amount for me.

"This bothers you because you're feeling guilty?" Evan asked.

"I guess so. I can't imagine that a cake that I sold for four hundred dollars four months ago is now worth two or three thousand dollars. It's crazy!"

"Abby, you don't decide what they should pay," Dad said. "They are. And wasn't that the whole point in the beginning?"

"I guess it was."

"Then I think you should just count your blessings, run your business the best you can, grow if you want, pay your workers well, and save a ton of money," Dad said. "This might not last forever, and someday you'll want it to slow down for a family. Make it count while you can."

If Dane had been here, he would have been comforted to see that my family knew what was important to me. They knew I'd never let the bakery keep me from having a family.

"So, Abby," Mom said, "anything new with you and Dane?" I felt the color rise in my cheeks. I took a bite of salad to delay a response. I'd expected someone to ask me about Dane, but it was difficult for me to think about him without feeling embarrassed and ashamed.

Kate looked at me closely and then came to my rescue. "And, Evan, what's up with you and Nicole?" I gave Kate an appreciative look.

"I think I might ask her to marry me."

Mom and Kate gasped. Dad laid down his fork and folded his hands, waiting to hear more. I nearly choked on my salad. Only Sam and Izzy seemed unsurprised.

"Really?" asked Kate. "Are you serious?"

"Why wouldn't I be? She's amazing. We get along great, and we want the same things. I'd be crazy not to."

"Are we talking soon?" I asked.

"Actually, yes. I've already found a ring I know she'll love, and I was thinking of asking her around Thanksgiving."

"When were you going to tell us?" I asked.

"Today," he said.

"Congratulations, son," said Dad. "She seems like a fine girl."

Quiet, private Evan surprised me. He told us how he was planning to ask Nicole and how he knew she was the right one. I'd never seen him so open about his feelings and plans. I was thrilled for him.

"Dane is starting the work on my house tomorrow. Did he tell you?" Evan asked, and I shook my head. I hadn't really given him a chance to tell me much of anything. "I called him last week and told him I wanted to get started now so we can get everything out of the way. Then we can concentrate on a wedding."

"That's so great," I said.

"I'm happy for you, Evan," Kate said. "Sam's been waiting a long time to have another in-law in the family."

"It's about time. It's been pretty rough," Sam said. Kate punched him in the arm.

"Do you like her family?" Mom asked.

"They're good people," Evan said.

"Have you talked to her father?" Dad asked.

"Yes. Her parents are happy for us."

"Are they okay with the short engagement?" Kate asked.

"They're fine. Neither of us want a long engagement. We both know what we want, and we're ready to move forward." A stab of jealousy pierced my heart. Shy Evan and Nicole talked more about things than Dane and I had. I wanted to go back to the beginning and ask more questions. I wanted to make Dane feel more comfortable asking me questions. I wanted us to share and be open so we wouldn't have a giant misunderstanding hanging over us. I couldn't wait to talk to Dane. I promised myself that when I saw him again, we wouldn't talk about cakes and business. We'd talk about hopes and dreams and plans.

"Abby." Evan interrupted my thoughts. "Nicole wants you to do the cake, of course."

"Of course," I said. "It will be your wedding gift from me."

I should have thought about Evan and Nicole and how happy I was for them, but instead the drive home was filled with thoughts of how much I missed Dane.

Twenty-seven

Peanut Butter Cake

1 cup flour
1 cup + 2 Tbsp. sugar
3½ tsp. baking powder
1 tsp. salt
1¼ cups peanut butter
2 cups graham cracker crumbs
1 cup + 2 Tbsp. milk
1 tsp. vanilla extract
3 eggs

Preheat oven to 375°F if baking with a metal dish, 325°F if using a glass dish.

Sift flour, sugar, baking powder, and salt together. Add peanut butter, graham cracker crumbs, milk, and vanilla. Beat with electric mixer on low until moistened and then beat on medium for 2 minutes. Add eggs and beat for 1 minute. Bake in greased, 9 x 13 pan for 30–35 minutes. Do not remove from pan to cool.

This was sitting by the front door," Lara said when she walked into the kitchen. In her hands were my silver cake plate and an envelope. The plate was the one I'd used for Dane's lemon and raspberry cream birthday cake.

The note excited me. I wished I'd had the chance to apologize first, but I was so happy he'd reached out that I didn't mind. I tried to control my enthusiasm. "Thanks, Lara," I said. I put the cake plate away and held the envelope to my heart. "I'll be in my office for a few minutes. Could you get started on the Martin cake?"

I closed my office door and sat down. I turned the envelope over in my hands. Suddenly I felt afraid to open it. Finally, I carefully tore open the envelope and unfolded the letter.

> *Dear Abby,*
>
> *I'm not sure what happened the other night. I went from feeling ready to ask you to marry me to feeling very confused about us.*
>
> *I'm happy for you that your business has grown. I know it was important to you that you not fail. I feel torn because I want you to succeed, but I feel like the bakery that brought us together is now tearing us apart. I can't compete with something that takes up all your time. If I can't compete, how will you fit in a family?*
>
> *I think you're amazing, Abby, and I want to have a future with you, but right now, I think you need to figure things out. You've placed so much importance on what something is worth, but I don't know if you've thought about how much we're worth. That's probably an important thing to figure out.*
>
> *I love you, and I miss you, but I think we need to take a little breather and figure things out.*
>
> *Love, Dane*

I read the letter again. I was yo-yoing between understanding and anger. Was this a breakup? Did he not want to talk about things? Were we not going to apologize and make up? By the time I'd read the letter a third time, I felt wretched. How could this be happening? This wasn't the way it was supposed to go. I'd been waiting to see him so I could tell him how sorry I was, but apparently I wasn't going to get the chance. We were taking a breather—one I hadn't asked for and seemed to have no say in. I put the note in my desk drawer and closed it firmly. It was a busy week, and I didn't have time to close myself up in my office sulking.

Days passed. Every day I thought about calling Dane or stopping by his house, but now I felt unwelcome. I was hurt that he'd so easily left me, and I was angry that his note had shut me out.

I tried to keep busy. I baked, decorated, and delivered cakes. I went through the books and was surprised to discover just how much money I was making. "Kate, you're not going to believe this," I said one afternoon on the phone. "I made over thirty-five thousand dollars last month."

"You're kidding," she said.

"Can you believe that? The month before that was only twenty-one thousand. It jumped over fourteen thousand in a month."

"Did you seriously just say 'only twenty-one thousand'?" Kate said. We laughed.

"Believe me, I know twenty-one thousand is great, but thirty-five? I can't even believe it. And I already have fourteen thousand for next month from people who wanted to pay in advance. Plus there are sixteen more bookings that haven't paid yet. This is crazy!"

"Did you ever imagine you'd be this successful?" Kate asked.

"Not in my wildest dreams. Lara and April are thrilled since I pay them a percentage instead of a flat salary."

"You do?"

"I figured it was the only fair way to do it. I couldn't make it without them, and if I'm paying what people are worth, it seems like the right thing to do."

"Wow, I'll bet they *are* thrilled. What other job would give them that kind of deal?"

"I don't mind. I want them to be happy here, and they're worth every penny I pay them."

"How's your new receptionist working out?"

"Kelly? She's fantastic."

"Do you pay her a percentage?"

"No. I'm paying her a salary with monthly bonuses."

"Maybe I should have applied for that job," Kate said. I knew she wasn't serious. "You're going to have to suggest to Dane that he might want to be Mr. Mom and let you bring home the bacon," Kate said. She was teasing, but her words were like a knife in my heart. I didn't say anything. "Abby, I was only kidding."

"I know you were," I said. I felt horrible. Since our fight, there had been so many things said that reminded me of how thoughtless I had been. I'd never stopped to think about how Dane felt. I wondered if I'd ever get a chance to tell him how I felt and how sorry I was.

"What do you think you'll do about the bakery when you get married and have kids?" Kate asked. "Will you just try to hire more help, or will you cut back the number of cakes you make? There's no way you can keep up this pace with kids."

"I don't have to worry about it until Dane proposes. *If* he proposes."

"Oh, please," Kate said. "We all know he's going to propose. I'm just surprised Evan is beating him to the punch. I thought Dane would ask you long before Evan got the nerve to ask Nicole."

"Sometimes people surprise you," I said. "Evan surprised me. I'm just glad he's so happy. And I love Nicole."

"He's going to be a great husband. And a dad," Kate said. I thought about Dane with Izzy and Ruby and Benjamin. He would be a great dad too.

"I know. He's wanted this for a long time." After I hung up the phone, I thought about my quiet, kind brother. He'd always loved kids. Ever since his mission, he'd wanted to start his family. He'd been disappointed a few times, but he'd been so happy since he met Nicole. Finally, at the age of twenty-seven, he'd found what he'd been waiting for. Twenty-seven. I hadn't realized he and Dane were the same age. Dane had said he'd been waiting a long time. Somehow it hadn't occurred to me that he and Evan were in the same boat. Since I'd watched Evan agonize over finding the right girl all these years, his search had seemed more urgent, more painful. Why hadn't I realized that Dane had felt the same?

I worked hard to distract myself. I didn't want to wallow in self-pity. Of course finding things to do during the day wasn't a problem. The problem was forcing myself not to obsess about Dane and our situation. I was cheerful and involved at work. I stayed occupied in the evenings reading books, catching up on movies I hadn't seen, visiting family, and going to bed earlier.

Sometimes I'd let myself think about Dane. I'd replay the good times in my mind. Then I'd replay that last day. I wondered when he would call. When would I see him again? How long did he want this breather to last, and should I wait him out or take the situation into my own hands and call him? I knew he had been working on the remodel at Evan's farm, and I felt jealous that Evan was probably seeing Dane every day. I wondered if Dane had said anything about us but decided he hadn't since Evan hadn't mentioned anything. I didn't say anything to anyone.

As more time passed, I worried that maybe our relationship was doomed to die from neglect. I didn't want it to end this way. I had no experience in the art of fighting and making up with boyfriends. I'd been waiting for Dane to take the lead. One evening, confused and torn, I decided if he wasn't going to call me, I'd have to call him. I picked up the phone and dialed his cell phone. It went immediately to voice mail. I listened to his voice, but when it gave me the signal to leave a message, I hung up. This wasn't something that could be done with a message. I tried again twice the next day, but both times it went directly to his voice mail. Another week ended with nothing resolved.

The next week was insanely busy. I tried to call once in the evening, but when it went to voice mail, I hung up. I didn't try again. I didn't want to be the only one who cared enough to try to make contact. I was so disappointed. Didn't he miss me? If he really loved me, wouldn't he see that I'd called and call me back? How could he let it end like this? Maybe the time and distance had made him realize he didn't love me after all. Maybe he felt relieved.

"Abby, your brother is on line one," Kelly said, leaning around the door. My first thought was to wonder when he'd last seen Dane.

"Hi, Evan."

"Hey, Abby, how are you?" he asked. I could tell by the sound of his voice that he wasn't casually asking me. He really wanted to know.

"I'm fine. How are you?" I thought I was doing a pretty good job of imitating a person who felt happy and normal.

"Are you? Fine, I mean?"

"Sure. Just busy, as usual. What's up?" I hoped he'd tell me something about Dane. It felt awful knowing that Evan knew more about Dane's life than I did.

"Well . . ." Evan hesitated. He'd never been one to pry into other people's lives. He was a private person and had always been respectful of the privacy of others.

"What is it, Evan? Just spit it out," I said.

"Okay, what's going on with you and Dane?"

"What did he say was going on?" I asked.

"He said you were taking a breather." I looked out my office window at the rose bushes. They looked barren, their faded, curling petals littering the ground around the bushes. I rested my forehead on the cool pane of glass. I felt betrayed that Dane had shared our situation with someone else.

Hearing the word "breather" come from Evan sounded so official. So final. It had been weeks since Dane and I had spoken. A breather? This felt like a pretty long breath.

"Uh, yeah." I didn't have any idea what to say.

"He said you're busy with the bakery and his uncle needs his help on a project in Portland, so it's a good time to take stock of things and see how you both feel later."

I felt like I'd been punched in the stomach. I fell into my chair.

"Abby, are you really okay with that?" Evan asked. I hated that he sounded so worried about me. It made it harder for me to hold myself together.

"Well . . . I guess so," I said.

So Dane was taking the job for his uncle. I'd given him no reason not to. I wished I could ask Evan when Dane was leaving and when he'd get back and what else he'd said about me and if he seemed happy. I didn't dare ask any of these things, so instead I said, "How does your house look? It's probably about finished, huh?" I knew I sounded wooden.

"Uh, it looks great. You should come out and see it. Dane's finishing it up this week, just before he heads to Portland." So soon. And I didn't know how long he'd be gone. I didn't want to ask anything that would let Evan know how completely in the dark I was about everything concerning Dane.

How could Dane do this without talking to me? Why hadn't he told me? Was our relationship really so shallow that it couldn't endure one fight?

One fight. As soon as those words crossed my mind, I knew it wasn't the fight we weren't enduring. It was the uncertainty of where our lives were taking us. Dane hadn't wanted a woman married to her job, and I had wanted a commitment before I changed things in my bakery. It was a horrible, damaging circle. I laid my head down on the desk, still holding the phone to my ear.

"Abby, did you hear me?" Evan asked.

"Sure, I'll come see it next week," I said. It would be hard to see the beautiful things Dane had done to Evan's place and know that Dane was probably out of my life for good. But I loved Evan, and I'd set aside my feelings to be supportive.

"That's not what I said."

"Oh, sorry. What did you say?"

"I asked you why you felt you needed a breather?"

"Did he say I needed the breather?" I asked.

"Well, he said you both did, but that you needed to sort a few things out."

"Wow. I thought we both had a few things to sort out." I didn't like feeling like this was all my fault. I knew my commitment to the bakery was a challenge, but Dane's reticence to talk to me about things had also been a problem. I was frustrated that he'd talked to Evan instead of me. And I was tired of how unpredictable my feelings were. One minute I was sad and sorry, recognizing the difficult situation Dane was in, and then the next I felt defensive and angry. The whole thing was driving me crazy.

"Look, Abby, I don't want to get in the middle of this," Evan said. "I just wanted to be sure you were okay."

"I am," I said. "Thanks for caring about me, Evan. You're a good brother. Now let's talk about something good. Are you getting excited? Does she suspect you're going to ask her at Thanksgiving?"

"Probably, but I haven't told her. I think she just suspects that it's coming soon. I can't believe Thanksgiving is almost here."

"Time flies," I said, a little absently.

"It sure does. How's business?" I couldn't help but smile. Evan was clearly more comfortable on these safe subjects.

"It's good. We have twenty-six cakes booked for December, and we've already scheduled quite a few into next year. But don't worry. We'll make sure we have time for yours. Let me know as soon as you set the date."

"We will."

"It's crazy. I've been paid over twenty thousand for December already, and I have a lot of bookings that haven't paid yet."

"Are you sure you can live on that?" Evan asked.

"It might cramp my Christmas giving a bit, but I'll try," I said. It felt good to be joking around with Evan. I hadn't laughed in weeks.

"It's been a meteoric rise," he said. "I'd never have imagined the day of the open house that you'd be this successful by year's end."

"I wouldn't have either. I wonder what Aunt Grace would think about all this."

"As long as you're happy, she'd be thrilled." I felt the breath catch in my throat. Of course, I loved that the bakery was so successful. This was a dream come true. But was I happy? I wasn't. And there was nothing I could do about it. I was taking a breather I'd never asked for.

"Thanks for calling me, Evan. I love you."

"I love you too, sis. Call me if you need anything." I hung up the phone and sat back in my chair. I didn't want Dane to go. I imagined conversations we could have that would solve all our problems. I imagined Dane asking me to marry him. Where would he have done it? On Alki Beach? On a Victoria bus? Or maybe somewhere we'd never been. I was completely unaware of time until Kelly leaned her head through the open door.

"I'm going to take off now," she said.

"Okay, have a nice evening," I said.

"Thanks. I will." She was studying my face. "Everything okay with your brother?"

"Everything's good. He's very happy."

"That's good. I'll see you tomorrow." I could tell she was hesitating. I appreciated her concern, but I didn't feel like talking, so I stood to go as well. Soon the door closed behind her, and I was alone in the bakery.

The call from Evan had triggered something inside me, and I felt lost and a little nostalgic. I walked into the kitchen. It was clean and sparkling. I remembered Dane leaning against the counters of the old kitchen, taking notes on that first day. I remembered struggling to take my eyes off him. I thought about the floors he'd polished before he showed them to me. I walked into the showroom, with its wood trim and antique door. The door is what did it. I touched the cold, stained glass. I ran my fingers along the carved leaves. I stood there at that beautiful, scarred, perfect door and realized what I'd lost. I couldn't breathe.

So much for a breather.

Two days later, I heard my cell phone ringing from my coat pocket in my office. I was in the middle of placing a thirty-inch circle of fondant on a peanut butter cake and couldn't stop to answer it. I laid the fondant out, smoothed it over the cake, and cut off the excess. When the cake was covered and smooth, I retrieved my phone and looked at the history. Dane had called, and the little message envelope was flashing.

I closed the door, sat down at my desk, and called my voice mail.

"Hi Abby." His voice sounded so good. I leaned back in the chair and closed my eyes "It's me. Sorry I missed you. I was just calling to say hi and tell you I've decided to take the job with my uncle in Portland. I think this is best for both of us right now." There was a long pause. I waited, hoping there was more. He sighed. "Well, I'll be in touch. Take care."

And he was gone.

Twenty-eight

Grandma's Flaky Piecrust

1¼ cups flour
¼ tsp. salt
½ cup shortening, chilled
2–3 Tbsp. ice water

Whisk the flour and salt together in a medium-sized bowl. With a pastry blender, cut in the cold shortening until the mixture resembles coarse crumbs. Drizzle 2–3 tablespoons ice water over mixture. Toss mixture with a fork to moisten, adding more water a few drops at a time until the dough comes together.

Gently gather dough particles together into a ball. Wrap in plastic wrap and chill for at least 30 minutes before rolling.

Roll out dough and put in a pie plate. Fill with desired filling and bake according to pie directions for a filled pie or at 350 degrees for twenty minutes.

Since I knew I'd see the family at Thanksgiving and I wasn't ready to answer any relationship questions, I avoided the Sunday family dinner in November. No one but Evan knew about our break, so no one was particularly worried when I said I couldn't make it. I hoped Evan wouldn't share anything.

Thanksgiving dinner was delicious, as it always was. I arrived early with the pumpkin pies and rolls. I'd taken over the pies and rolls several years ago, but with my bakery kitchen, this year they'd taken much less time.

I helped Mom set the table with a dark green tablecloth and the good china that had been used for Thanksgiving and Christmas dinners since before I was born. We ate in the early afternoon, enjoying perfect turkey and all the fixings. The atmosphere was warm and comfortable, and everyone visited and laughed throughout the meal. Izzy, now three, ate at the big people table and used the big people manners Kate had been teaching her.

After dinner, we cleaned up and gathered in the living room to participate in the gratitude circle. This was as much a part of Thanksgiving as the food. We'd gather together and each person would share something they were thankful for. It had evolved over the years, with gratitude for bicycles and good math scores being replaced by blessings a little more profound. Dad started.

"I'd just like to express my gratitude for the wonderful events of this last year. All my children are living lives that make them happy and are experiencing great success. That is always a relief for a father." He paused and reached for Mom's hand. "And of course I'm thankful for your mother. She's a wonderful partner, and I wouldn't want to go through this life with anyone else." I felt a little ache in my heart.

Mom smiled and squeezed Dad's hand before starting. "This year I'm thankful for so many things, I'm having a hard time narrowing it down. But I'd like to say that I'm so thankful that my kids have found wonderful spouses," she said, looking at Sam. "Fiancées," she said, looking at Nicole, who had been sporting a beautiful ring since last night. "And boyfriends," she said, looking at me. "We're just sorry Dane couldn't be here." I was relieved that Evan hadn't said anything to Mom and Dad. I smiled at her and felt like a liar. They didn't know. I felt Evan looking at me and wondered what he was thinking. I didn't dare meet his eyes.

"Abby?" Dad said. I took a deep breath.

"I don't even know where to start. I guess I could narrow it all down by saying I'm thankful for Aunt Grace for making this entire last year happen. So I'd have to probably leave it there. Thanks for Aunt Grace."

I knew everyone expected something a little different, or more, but I turned to Sam, who was after me, letting everyone know I was finished.

Izzy was asleep on Sam's lap. "I'd have to say I'm thankful for my family. I don't know how I got so lucky to find such a wonderful wife and mom for Izzy and Olivia or Jonathan, whichever it turns out to be." It took a moment for what he'd said to register.

"What did you say?" Mom asked.

Sam and Kate smiled, and Kate nodded.

"Are you kidding?" I asked. "When?"

"The end of May," Kate said.

"And you haven't told us?" Evan asked.

"We thought this would be a fun way to announce it," Kate said. After a short break to exchange hugs and congratulations, Dad asked Kate to continue the gratitude circle.

"I'd have to agree with Abby. I'm so thankful for Aunt Grace's generosity. We love our home and we're so happy there. So I'm thankful for Aunt Grace."

Then it was Evan's turn. "At the beginning of the year, I'd have said the farm was the greatest blessing of my year, but since something even better than the farm has happened, I'd have to say I'm thankful to Aunt Grace too. Without her, I wouldn't have been living in North Bend and I wouldn't have met Nicole. Aunt Grace gave me more than she realized." I nodded in agreement. Until recently, I'd been so grateful that Aunt Grace's gift had given me the bakery and had allowed me to meet Dane. The pain in my heart right now was making me question whether meeting Dane had been a blessing or a curse. I didn't know if I could live with this loss.

"I'm seeing a theme, here," Dad said. "Nicole?"

"I'm thankful for Evan. I couldn't have asked for a better man to marry. It's been a great year."

"Amen," Dad said, and the others echoed their agreement. No one noticed that I didn't join in. Except maybe Evan. But since I couldn't look at him, I would never be sure.

A short time later, a strange thing happened. Sam and Kate took Izzy to visit Sam's family, and Evan and Nicole left to spend the evening with Nicole's family. "Well, this is a first," Mom said. "It's just us tonight. What shall we do?"

"Let's watch a movie," I said. I didn't want to think any more. I just wanted to lose myself in a movie and not have to do too much talking. I couldn't bear any questions tonight. It was painfully clear to me that my brother and sister's lives were moving forward and mine wasn't.

"How about the BBC *Pride and Prejudice*," Mom said "We haven't seen that in ages, and when, other than Thanksgiving, can you justify sitting and watching a movie for nearly six hours."

So we watched *Pride and Prejudice*, and my heart hurt all evening. For the first time in my life, I felt resentment toward Elizabeth. She got Mr. Darcy. They loved each other enough to set aside their pride. When the movie was over, I gathered my empty dishes, kissed Dad and Mom good-bye, and went home to my empty house.

Twenty-nine

See's Fudge

4½ cups sugar
1 can evaporated milk
5 cups semisweet chocolate chips
½ pound butter
2 cups nuts
1 tsp. vanilla

Mix sugar with evaporated milk. Bring to a rolling boil for 7 to 8 minutes, stirring often.

In a large bowl, mix together chocolate chips and butter.

Pour hot sugar mixture over chocolate mixture. After chocolate has melted, add nuts and vanilla.

Blend well, pour into buttered pan, and chill in refrigerator.

December roared in, bringing a Christmas season full of beautiful, wintry weddings. So far, I'd never dealt with any major delivery issues, other than the usual Seattle rainstorms. But December blew in with a flurry and the flurries stayed. Snow rarely stays on the ground more than a day or two in Seattle, but this year, it snowed and then it snowed again and then it kept snowing. It altered our patterns of delivery, and we had to leave a lot more time to get where we were going.

On December 3, Lara and I were delivering a beautiful white cake covered with royal icing snowflakes. We started climbing a fairly steep hill to a gothic church, complete with gargoyles and moss on the roof. A third of the way up, the car slowed to a stop. I tried not to panic as we slid backward to stop against the snowy curb. I backed up the van and we tried again but only made it a few feet farther than the first time.

The car wasn't going to make it, and the church was still too far away for us to deliver the cake on foot. We'd never had a problem with delivery before, and a feeling of panic settled in. How were we going to deliver this cake?

Lara called her boyfriend, Jason, and asked if he could come meet us at the bottom of the hill and carry the cake up to the wedding in his SUV. It was the first time I'd questioned the purchase of a minivan for my deliveries. Thank goodness we'd given ourselves plenty of time. Once Jason arrived, we abandoned the car for an hour and safely delivered the cake. The next day I gave Lara a check for one hundred dollars to give to Jason.

"He won't want that," she said. "He didn't mind coming."

"I know he didn't," I said, "but he saved me from disaster."

"The trip wasn't worth a hundred bucks," she insisted.

"It was worth it to me," I said. "Just take it to him. Please."

"All right," Lara said. "You know, Jason said if you had studded snow tires, you'd have been able to make it up that hill. I mean, that might seem extreme for Seattle, but since you deliver cakes, I don't know. Maybe it would be a good idea."

"It's a great idea," I said. By the end of the day, both minivans were sporting studded snow tires, and Jason was right. I didn't have another weather-related problem with a delivery during the entire snowy winter.

Buying Christmas presents should have been a breeze. I had more money than I'd ever had. I enjoyed picking out presents for my family and my bakery staff. But the task felt unfinished. I wanted to shop for Dane. I'd been planning for months what I'd give him—a new iPod with our favorite music and a new dress shirt and sweater. I felt restless and fretful. I even thought about getting him the presents anyway, but not knowing how he'd feel about receiving them, I didn't have the courage.

⁓◦◦◦⁂◦◦◦⁓

One night, as I watched Jeopardy and warmed up a bowl of soup, the phone rang.

"Hello."

"Hi. Is this Abby Benson?"

I didn't recognize the man's voice.

"Yes, it is."

"This is Brad Dennelly."

The name sounded vaguely familiar, but I couldn't put a face with it. "Brad Dennelly?"

"Yes. You know, from the ward."

"Oh, hi Brad." I still didn't know who I was speaking to. He must have heard the confusion in my voice.

"I sat in front of you in Sunday School last week. I made the comment about carrying out our priesthood responsibilities by dating regularly until we find 'the one,' " he said. Now I knew who it was, and it didn't make me particularly happy.

"Oh yes, now I remember. How are you?" I asked.

"I'm fine. Thanks for asking. I heard through the grapevine that you're back on the market, and I thought to myself, 'Oh my heck, you've got to ask her out right away.' " I cringed and slouched down on the couch so that my feet would reach the coffee table. "So is it true? Are you back on the market?" I wasn't sure which phrase I hated more—"oh my heck" or "on the market."

"Well, probably not exactly on the market," I said.

"What would you say you are?"

"I'm not sure exactly."

"Well, as long as you're not engaged, or close to being engaged, I was hoping we could go to the stake Christmas choral concert Sunday after next. I have a friend in the choir, and he says it's going to be real nice. They're going to have excellent refreshments, and who doesn't like Christmas music? Anyway, I thought, 'Ask that Abby Benson. She probably likes Christmas music and good refreshments.' Was I right? Do you like Christmas music?"

"Um, sure. I like Christmas music."

"And I imagine since you own a bakery, you're not one of those girls who doesn't like refreshments." Could this conversation be more awkward? I wondered if I should be amused or offended by his comments. It didn't really matter. I knew I didn't want to go with him. But I had no legitimate excuse, and the poor guy was trying so hard, I couldn't bring myself to say no.

"You know, Brad, I'm not engaged, so I guess a Christmas concert would be fine."

"Well. What. Do. You. Know. I had a feeling I should call you, and I was right." Ugh. He might have had a good feeling about it, but I definitely didn't.

It had been nearly two months since I'd spoken to Dane. Over seven weeks of this emotional roller coaster. There were the defensive hills, where I knew if he'd asked me more questions, he'd have known I was willing to set aside everything for a good husband and children. Then would come the repentant valleys. I'd realize I'd been so focused on the success of the bakery that I'd never let him know where my priorities were. I wanted off the roller coaster. I wanted some sanity. I was tired of the "whys" and "what-ifs" that ran constantly through my mind. I needed some peace, and the only way I could get it was to try to set aside the entire mess and get through the holidays.

I wanted to be happy, and I didn't want to be a wet blanket as Evan and Nicole planned their wedding. I would no longer get wrapped up in thinking about Dane and what might have been.

Two days into my fresh resolve, I was doing pretty well. Then one afternoon Kelly laid the mail on my desk. On top was a Christmas card with a Portland postmark. I knew who it was from, and suddenly I could hear my heart beating in my ears. I looked at every other piece of mail before I returned to the red envelope with the Portland postmark. Then I slowly opened it.

Inside was a card with a picture of the baby Jesus on the front. It had an embossed silver border. I opened the card and read.

Abby,

Merry Christmas. I hope you're doing well and that next year brings you everything you want. I'm busy working on my uncle's house. It's a beautiful old place. I'll be here until some time in January. Then I'll be back in Seattle working with Dad and Blake. It's been nice working with my uncle.

Well, I miss you.

Take care.

Dane

Welcome back to the roller coaster. After seven weeks of nothing, it was good to get something. But it was so cool, so reserved. But at least he had sent a card. That was more than I had done. But it said so little. What was he feeling? Was he sad at all? He said he missed me, but I longed for more. How much did he miss me, or had he thrown that in there so it wouldn't sound so distant?

Did the card mean anything? *Just call him. He sent the card. He broke the ice.* Would it be okay for me to call him? My heart couldn't take this—not just the part that loved and missed Dane, but the part of my heart that was threatening to explode. I picked up my cell phone and started dialing his number.

"Abby, LilaBeth DeGraffio is here for her appointment," Kelly said over the intercom. I clicked the off button on my phone and walked out to meet with LilaBeth.

The best thing about decorating wedding cakes is that once you know what you're doing, you can practically decorate in your sleep. I had spent many hours pondering life and its complexities while Swiss dotting a wedding cake. I had watched movies while forming marzipan roses, and countless hours of prayer and problem-solving had taken place while I carefully placed mosaic tile fondant pieces into a buttercream concrete.

The worst thing about decorating cakes is that once you know what you're doing, you can practically decorate in your sleep. The day of Angela Peterson's stained glass poinsettia cake had arrived, and for about ten straight hours, I etched the outlines of poinsettias on the cake with a toothpick. Then I outlined each tiny section of the picture with black royal icing that mimicked the leading. I carefully mixed food coloring with piping gel and painted each petal and leaf and stamen. When one layer was painted, I would set it aside and move on to the next. When the last layer was finished, the first layer was dry.

As I brought the fondant canvas to life, I had way too much time to think. For the first few hours, I had Lara and April's cheerful banter to keep me company, but at four o'clock, they left to deliver a cake while I stayed behind and finished painting. I still had about five more hours of work. I was in the zone, so I worked late into the evening, painting, thinking, reliving every conversation, every kiss, every wonderful moment of my ten months with Dane. Missing him was a physical ache. I couldn't bring myself to think about the fight. My trip down memory lane stopped just before his birthday.

When the last layer of the cake was painted, I cleaned up the kitchen, locked the doors, and went home. I felt sad and lonely. I told myself this was probably the wrong time to try to call Dane again, but my loneliness overtook my better judgment, and I dialed his number. I tried to control my shortness of breath as the phone rang.

"Hello?" a man's voice said. It didn't sound like Dane.

"Um, hi. Is this Dane?"

"No, this is his uncle. He must have left his phone here when he went out tonight. Can I take a message for him?"

"No, that's okay. I'll just try him another time," I said.

I hadn't cried myself to sleep for a couple of weeks, but questions tormented me. Where was he and who was he with? After my lonely day and the disappointment of the phone call, my tears soaked my pillow by the time I finally fell asleep.

"Wow! That cake is incredible," April said the next morning as I put the dowels in each layer. April was mixing cakes, and Lara was piping royal icing polka dots.

"Were you a painter in another life?" Lara asked.

"Not that I'm aware of." I stepped back to take a look. I wouldn't stack the four layers until I arrived at the wedding, but even in their unfinished condition, they were impressive. I was pleased with how they looked and felt more like an artist than I ever had. This would be a fun delivery. I always felt a little thrill when I knew I was leaving a masterpiece, and this was definitely one of those deliveries.

I delivered the cake to the Four Seasons Hotel. I had never been inside the Four Seasons before, and I was eager to see the inside of the modern glass and stone structure. At the service entrance I was met by a young man in a suit.

"I have a wedding cake for the Peterson wedding," I said through my window.

"Pull the car right over there and we'll get you a cart. We'll park your car for you."

"Thanks." I pulled into the designated spot. I wished Lara or April or Kate could have come with me. This was fun. I'd never been valet parked while delivering a cake before. Moments later, a cart was beside the car, and I carefully transferred the four tiers and supplies.

"When you're finished, just come to this door and we'll retrieve your car for you," the young man said. I wheeled the cart inside the wide automatic doors. Inside the entrance, a map of the hotel directed me to the ballroom.

I stopped breathing for a moment when I saw the room. I'd set up cakes in some beautiful settings before, but I'd never seen anything like this. An entire wall of windows overlooked the water. It was a wide and picturesque vista. The tables were set with delicate china, and the room was an explosion of flowers. The centerpiece for each table was a blooming amaryllis in a crystal pot. The walls on either end of the windows were trellised with poinsettias—not scattered poinsettias, but solid walls of poinsettias that looked like a wall of rich, three-dimensional wallpaper. Suspended from the ceiling were giant balls hanging from wide, green grosgrain ribbons. They looked like upside-down topiary trees in pink, white, and red roses. Walt Disney himself couldn't have imagined such an exquisite scene.

I found the cake table situated in front of one of the walls of flowers and began to set up the cake. I centered the ornate, silver cake stand and carefully stacked the cakes, adding a tiny black bead border around the bottom of each tier. It gave the impression that the stained glass moved easily from one tier to the next.

I completed the setup by placing a few sprigs of evergreen around the base of the cake stand and stepped back to survey the work. I was completely happy with how it looked, so I took my photos and headed for the door.

"Abby?" I turned around to see a pretty woman walking quickly toward me. "Are you Abby?" As she got closer, I could tell she was the bride's mother—an elegant, older version of the bride herself.

"I am." I turned and shook her outstretched hand. "This is gorgeous. The flowers are amazing."

"Oh, thank you. I just walked by the cake, and it is magnificent. Absolutely stunning. When Angela described the cake as looking like stained glass, I couldn't really picture it, but I knew it would be lovely. I saw your work on television."

"Oh, thank you," I said.

"Abby, this exceeds my wildest expectations. I've never seen anything like it."

"I'm glad you like it. I hope Angela will be happy with it."

"Oh my, she's going to be thrilled. Anyway, let me go ahead and pay you while you're here." She reached into her beaded evening bag.

"Angela already paid me," I said.

"Oh no, she just paid you the deposit."

"Actually, I'm sure she paid me the full amount. She's already paid two thousand," I said.

Mrs. Peterson patted my arm. "Abby, even if Angela thought she was paying the full amount, that cake over there is not a two-thousand-dollar cake. I've got the rest of your money right here." She tucked an envelope into my hand. "Now you have a wonderful Christmas." She air kissed me and then turned and walked back across the room. I stood there a little dazed. First, I couldn't believe she was paying me more, and second, I'd never been air kissed before.

I wheeled the cart back to the service entrance, and a different man brought my car around to me. I had made a habit of prolonging the suspense of each payment by waiting until I was back at the bakery, sitting at my desk, before I opened the envelope. It was hard to keep my mind from running wild, and I kept glancing over at the envelope sitting on the passenger seat as I drove home.

At the bakery, I carried in the supplies and washed and put away the icing bag, bowl, and tips before I walked into my office and sat down at the desk. Finally, I opened the envelope. Inside was a check for six thousand more dollars. Would I ever consider my cakes worth what others were willing to pay?

Thirty

Lemon Kiss Cookies

1½ cups butter
¾ cup sugar
3 Tbsp. lemon juice
2¾ cups flour
1½ cups almonds, finely chopped in blender or
    food processor
1 (14-oz.) pkg. milk chocolate candy kisses
powdered sugar
1 Tbsp. shortening
½ cup chocolate chips

In large bowl, beat butter, sugar, and lemon juice until light and fluffy. Add flour and almonds; beat at slow speed until well mixed. Cover and refrigerate at least 1 hour for easier handling.

Heat oven to 375°F. Shape a tablespoon full of dough around each chocolate kiss, covering it completely. Roll in hand to form ball. Place on ungreased cookie sheet and bake for 8–12 minutes or until set and the edges are lightly, golden brown.

After removing from oven allow to partially cool on baking sheet until firm enough to lift (about 10 minutes), then cool on racks completely. Lightly dust cookies with powdered sugar.

In small pan, melt chocolate chips and shortening; stir until smooth. Drizzle over each cookie.

$\mathcal{I}$'d already called Mom and Kate to tell them about my eight-thousand-dollar cake. Too tired to cook, I made myself a peanut butter sandwich for dinner. I sat down with my sandwich to watch an old episode of *The $25,000 Pyramid* on the Game Show Network. I knew it was a little crazy to watch people play a game they actually played decades ago, but I liked seeing the old styles of hair and clothes and wondering how the winners spent their money. Besides, it was mindless and cheerful, two things I needed right then. Just as Dick Clark was leading the contestant and her unknown-to-me celebrity partner to the winner's circle, my phone rang.

"Hello."

"Hey, Abby. How are you?" I recognized Dane's voice instantly and quickly turned off the television. I no longer cared whether or not Joyce from 1975 won twenty-five thousand dollars.

"Hi." I swallowed my bite of peanut butter sandwich and hoped the peanut butter on the roof of my mouth didn't make me sound like a cartoon character. "I'm fine. How are you?"

"Pretty good. My uncle said you called last night. Is everything okay?"

"Sure. I just got your Christmas card. I wanted to say thanks."

"Oh. No problem." There was a long pause. "So how is business going?"

"It's good. We've had some neat cakes." I didn't want to talk about the bakery. I didn't want to tell him we'd been super busy or that we were making loads of money. The bakery had been a big part of our problem. If I told him all that, maybe he'd think this separation should be permanent. "What about you?"

"I've just been working on my uncle's house. It's a really great place."

"Be sure to take some pictures. I'd love to see some before and afters." How could I keep the conversation going? His voice sounded so good. "Are you coming home for Christmas?" Please say yes.

"Actually, Blake is spending Christmas with Sarah's family, so Dad and Mom are going to come down here for Christmas."

"Oh," I said, disappointed. "That'll be nice."

"We'll be finishing up this house sometime in January, and then I'll be coming home. I'm looking forward to my own house instead of a tiny guest room."

"I'll bet you've missed your house. Evan's place looks great," I said.

"Oh, you've seen it?"

"I drove up Sunday before last. You made some great changes. I loved the kitchen."

"He asked Nicole for a lot of advice on the kitchen. She had some good ideas. They seem really happy."

"Yeah, they are."

"He deserves it." I suddenly felt sad. Dane deserved to be happy too. So did I. Why did things have to be so hard?

"When are you doing McKenzie Merriweather's cake?"

"In January."

"I'll bet that's pretty exciting."

"It is." At the moment, I didn't care at all about McKenzie Merriweather's cake or my trip to California or even baking in the Culinary Institute. I just wanted Dane back.

"That's good." There was a long pause. The air was full of unsaid things. I could feel us pulling away. We were protecting ourselves. We couldn't let our conversation drift too close to what might hurt. But one thing was long overdue, and I needed to say it.

"Dane, I'm sorry." My voice cracked a little. I didn't want him to know I was crying.

"It's okay."

"No, it isn't. I was terrible. I said—"

"Hey," he interrupted. "Everything happens for a reason. I needed to come do this job for my uncle, and we both had things we needed to figure out. Don't be so hard on yourself." Why did he need to go do that job? Had something important happened while he was there? And what did he mean we *had* things we needed to work out. Did the past tense mean we were really, finally, definitely over?

"I just wanted you to know I'm sorry," I said.

"I know. So am I." Again the long, heavy silence. "Well, I should go."

"Okay," I said. I knew I couldn't prolong the conversation without talking about things I might not want to hear. I wasn't ready for that. "Thanks for calling."

"Thanks for calling last night. I'll talk to you later."

"Bye." Would we ever talk to each other again? I felt worse than before we'd talked. Now I had so many questions. I replayed the conversation and couldn't find anything in it that gave me hope for our future. I put my sandwich on the coffee table. My stomach was in my throat, and I knew I couldn't possibly choke down food.

Then the phone rang again. I was so excited that Dane was calling back that I didn't even look at the caller ID. "Hello?" Maybe he was calling to tell me he still loved me and that we were going to be okay.

"Hey, Abby, what's chillin'? This is Brad."

"Oh." I sank back into the couch. "Hi, Brad."

"Just calling to let you know what time I'm picking you up tomorrow."

"Great." I longed for some way to get out of the date.

"We have two choices. I can pick you up at six and we can go straight to the performance, or, better yet, you could just come home with me from church tomorrow, and we could have dinner and hang out before we go. Whatta ya think?"

"Oh, well . . ." My mind was racing. I had to think of an excuse. Fast. "Actually, I think I'm going to church with my parents tomorrow. But I'll be back by six, so the first option will probably work out better for me."

"Well, that's too bad. I fix a mean pot of spaghetti."

"Sorry," I said, even though I wasn't.

"Well, another time then. I'll be by at six."

"Six it is."

"See ya tomorrow." I hung up the phone and buried my head in one of the couch pillows, wishing I could die on the spot and not have to face tomorrow.

I didn't go to church with my parents. I love the people in their ward, and they love me. They watched me grow up. They were there when I gave my first talk, and they put their arms around me when I foolishly agreed to sing a solo and then couldn't find the right note. I ended up singing most of the song off-key. I sat down humiliated and swore if anyone told me I'd sounded good I would never go to that ward again. After the meeting, Sister Bannock hugged me and told me not to feel bad. The piano doesn't carry very well, and it's really hard to hear the key from that spot on the stand. I was still humiliated, but I loved her for being honest with me.

But it was that love and honesty that scared me too. I didn't want questions from well-meaning people who'd want to know if I was dating, when I was getting married, and all the things home-ward people who care about you think they should know.

So instead of going to church with my parents, I drove out to Marysville and went to church in a ward where I didn't know anyone and no one would ask me hard questions and no one would want to fix me a pot of spaghetti. Only one elderly woman spoke to me, and that was to ask if the seat beside me was saved in Relief Society. The solitude was a luxury. After church, I drove around aimlessly. I didn't realize where I was driving until I saw Dane's house up ahead. Feeling like a teenage stalker, I drove home just in time to make myself a bowl of oatmeal and brush my teeth before Brad arrived.

"Hey, good-lookin'," he said. Ugh. Brad was about six feet tall and weighed about a hundred and forty pounds. He was a string bean with curly brown hair that flopped in his eyes.

"Hi, Brad." I locked the door behind me as we left.

"Did you have a nice day?"

"I did. Thanks."

"How's the fam?"

"They're all doing fine."

"Good to hear. So tell me about your bakery. I hear you're pretty famous."

I gave him the abridged version of the bakery, and he ooed and aahed in all the right places. I felt a little sorry for him. He was trying to be a good date. Trying way too hard.

We were early. Only a few people sat in the chapel. We took seats near the middle of the room, and I looked through the program.

"So, Abby, how long you been back on the market?" Really? Did he really think I wanted to talk about this? Here? With him?

"Oh, I don't know. I'm not really sure where things stand," I said. I didn't want to give him any false encouragement.

"Tell me about it," he said. His voice was earnest, and he put his arm on the back of the bench and leaned in close.

"I'm not sure there's much to tell," I said.

"Alright-y. But listen, Abby, when you're ready to talk, I'm here for you. I have to say, I was pretty glad to hear you weren't dating anyone anymore. I don't want to embarrass you, but I've had my eye on you for a while now."

"That's sweet," I said. I really didn't know how to respond to any of this. I couldn't remember feeling this uncomfortable on a date. Even Jerry eyeing the waitress was better than this. At least he wasn't making unwanted advances. Then Brad's hand came off the back of the bench and began caressing my arm. Up and down, up and down. "I'll be back in just a minute." I quickly stood and made my escape to the restroom.

Please, let this end.

Let this end.

Let. This. End!

I wished I'd never agreed to this evening. Why was I putting myself through this? I waited until just a minute before the concert was to begin, then went back out and sat by Brad, leaving as much space between us as I could. During a song about Mary's love for her baby, Brad slid a little closer and put his arm on the back of the bench again, but thankfully, this time he kept it on the bench and not on me.

Amen had barely been said when Brad was out of his seat. "Come on, I want you to meet my friend, Dan. He's the one who was in the choir." Brad grabbed my hand and led me to the cultural hall where tables were set up with refreshments. I didn't want to hold his hand, so I pulled it free and pretended to look for something in my purse.

"Dan, this is the pretty lady I was telling you about."

"Hey, pretty lady," Dan said.

"It's actually Abby," I said.

"Hey, pretty Abby," Dan said. He slugged Brad's arm, and the two of them got a good chuckle. "Brad's been telling me all about you." How could he tell him all about me? He didn't know me.

"I hope it was nice." Why was I having such a hard time with meaningless pleasantries? I just wanted to go home.

"Oh, it was nice, all right," he said, winking. Was this a joke? I looked around, wondering if someone was pulling a prank on me. Did people really talk like this?

"Of course it was nice. Like I said, I've had my eye on you."

"Why don't we go get a cookie or something to drink?" I said.

"A cookie sounds great," said Dan. Soon I was at the refreshment table, flanked by Brad and Dan.

"Shall we go find a seat? Sit and shoot the breeze for awhile?" Brad was a master of cliché's, and it appeared he planned to use them all tonight.

"Sounds good to me," said Dan. "How did you like the concert?"

"It was very nice. I love Christmas music," I said.

"I almost wished I was up there singing with you," Brad said, "but then I wouldn't have been sitting by the prettiest girl in the room," he said.

"But you coulda looked at her," Dan said. "I had a great view of her." Oh help.

When I'd finished my cookie—a delicious lemon and chocolate concoction—and punch, I theatrically wadded up the napkin and shoved it in my empty paper cup. "Well, gentlemen, I'm going to go throw this away, and then I think I should probably be getting home. I have a pretty big day ahead of me tomorrow."

"Making wedding cakes?" Brad asked.

"Yep, making wedding cakes." I stood and put my hand out. "It was nice meeting you, Dan."

"Oh, he's coming with us. I'm giving him a ride home. I hope you don't mind," Brad said. "We can make other arrangements if you'd rather go just the two of us."

"Oh no, no, no. That's just fine," I said. On the way out of the building, I snagged another cookie. They were so delicious, they were almost worth dealing with Brad and Dan. Almost.

At the car, Brad opened the door for me, and I got in at the same time as Dan.

"He really likes you, you know. He's got big plans," Dan said from the backseat as Brad walked around to the driver's side. Thankfully, he opened the door, sparing me the task of coming up with a response to that unwelcome bit of information. "Are you going to make your own wedding cake?" Dan asked.

"I haven't really thought about it," I said.

"Do you think we could come in and have a tour of the bakery?" Brad asked.

"Would another time be okay? I really do have to get up early in the morning."

"Sure thing." Dan and Brad visited the rest of the way home.

I opened the car door and stepped out as soon as the car came to a stop. "Good night. Thanks."

"Surely you're going to let me be a gentleman and walk you to the door," Brad said.

"Okay," I said, and we walked back to my house.

I unlocked the door. "Have a . . ." I started turning to him just in time to catch him coming in for a kiss. I turned my head quickly so that he just grazed my ear with his lips.

"Oh," he said. He took a step back, an expression of surprise on his face. "Uh, thanks for coming. I'll give you a call."

"Good night." I closed the door behind me and leaned against it. *Never again*, I thought. I should not have to endure evenings like this. I did not have to date anyone I didn't want to. I wiped off my ear on my sleeve and locked the door.

Thirty-one

Sunshine Dinner Rolls

1 (¼-oz.) package yeast
½ cup warm water
⅓ cup + 1 Tbsp. sugar (divided use)
1 tsp. baking powder
1 cup milk
⅓ cup butter
dash of salt
2 eggs, beaten
4½ cups flour

Dissolve yeast in warm water and add 1 tablespoon sugar and baking powder. Allow to stand for 20 minutes.

Meanwhile, scald milk. Add butter, ⅓ cup sugar, and salt. (This can be done in a glass 4-cup measuring cup in the microwave.) Cool a little and then add eggs.

Mix everything together with the flour. Cover and refrigerate overnight. (The dough will more than double in bulk, so make sure your container is big enough. If it looks like it might outgrow its bowl, you can always punch it down once or twice with no problem.)

Break off into pieces about the size of a small lemon and form into a ball. Place on a greased baking sheet about an inch apart. Cover with clean kitchen towels and allow to rise to close to double in size.

Bake at 425°F for 8–10 minutes. Mom always rubbed the
hot rolls with a stick of butter when they came out of the oven
to soften the tops and give them a beautiful sheen.

I never really got the opening line of Dickens's classic, even when we
studied it in high school. It's ironic that I had to live through it to
really understand it, but that year, it was the best of Christmases and it
was the worst of Christmases.

I wanted to have some sort of staff Christmas party, but we were
busy up until December 23, so two nights before Christmas, after our
last cake delivery, Kelly and her husband, Jim; Lara and Jason; and
April and I went out for dinner. I'm sure April could have rustled up a
date, but she was thoughtful and said if Dane was still going to be out
of town, then the two of us should go together. I didn't argue with her.
Kelly and Lara offered to come alone, but I didn't want to deny them a
nice evening out just because of me. No one knew what was happening
between Dane and me, although I imagine they had their suspicions.

We met at 13 Coins, a restaurant Lara had recommended. It was
elegant and plush, and from our table we had a great view of the chefs
preparing the meals in the open kitchen. I loved watching them work,
moving smoothly and easily around the giant stove, preparing meals
that looked more like art than food. It was a cheerful meal. Everyone
was happy and festive.

"You've got to tell Jim about the dotted Swiss cake last week," Kelly
said.

"Well," I said, "it was a three-tiered cake with about a million tiny
dots on it, like the size of the head of a pin. April and I had spent most
of the day just on the dots."

"I've never had such a cramp in my hand." April shook out her
hand to add emphasis.

"So we drove it over to the Edgewater Hotel and got it all set up,
but the flowers hadn't arrived yet, and they wanted us to put the flowers on the cake. The wedding planner told us the flowers were on their
way and would be there in about half an hour. She begged us to wait
for them. We were thirsty, and we didn't want to just sit there waiting,
so we walked through the lobby and found a place to buy a bottled

water. About twenty minutes later, we went back to put the flowers on the cake, and there was a little girl about four years old, standing by the cake, delicately picking off the little dots and sticking them in her mouth."

"At first I couldn't see what she was doing," April said. "I just thought it was a cute little girl in a pretty dress admiring the cake. I even said, 'Oh, look how cute.' But then we got closer, and I realized what she was doing. Then it wasn't very funny."

"She had pulled off about two or three hundred of those tiny little dots, and she'd put her finger clear through the fondant and into the cake in two places while she was doing it," I said.

"You should have seen her," said April. "A vandal in a cute, plaid Christmas dress with her hair piled up in curls on her head. She just smiled when we walked up. She didn't have any idea she was doing anything wrong."

"I asked her where her mom was just about the same time as her mom came racing into the room shrieking, 'Ashlyn, get away from the cake. Get away from the cake right now.' She was freaking out."

"Abby tried to tell the mom that it was okay, but she hurried the little girl out of there, chewing her out the entire time. I'm sure she was in a ton of trouble."

"Luckily we were both there because even with two of us working on the cake, it took about forty-five minutes to fix it," I said.

"And let me tell you," April said, "it isn't very easy to work together on something like that when the tiers are already stacked. We were practically working on top of each other. It felt like we were working with giant foam sports hands."

"What did you do about the holes?" Jason asked.

"We placed the flowers very strategically," I said.

I was glad we'd squeezed in a Christmas gathering. The stresses of the bakery were forgotten for the evening, and everyone was cheerful and relaxed.

After dessert, I raised my hand to get everyone's attention. "I'm not good at speeches, but I just have a few things I want to say to all of you. First of all, a year ago, this bakery was just a dream. Now it's a busy, successful place, and I couldn't have done it without each of you. I'm so grateful for the good year we've had, and I want you to know how glad I am to have each of you working with me. And I consider you all friends. This last year has been an interesting experiment, and I've learned a lot about the worth of things, and I can honestly say, you three are worth more than I could possibly pay you."

"So are you laying us off?" Lara asked. Everyone laughed.

"No, and you'd better not even think about quitting either. Honestly, you've all been amazing, so even though I think you're priceless, I've got a little something that I hope will show you how much I appreciate you." Everyone at the table smiled and clapped for me as I handed thick, heavy Christmas cards to Lara, April, and Kelly.

"Should we open them now?" Lara asked, lifting the corner of the flap to peek inside.

"I don't care when you open them," I said.

"Let's open them now," April said.

The three of them tore open the envelopes and pulled out their gifts.

"What on earth . . ." Kelly said. In her hand was a stack of fifty hundred-dollar bills.

"Abby, you didn't have to do this. You pay us great already," Lara said.

"Merry Christmas," I said.

"Merry Christmas to you too," April said. "Can I work for you next year too?"

I laughed. "I'm planning on it."

I felt great when I got home that night and put away the first edition copy of *Gone With the Wind* from Kelly, the cashmere hat and scarf from April, and the two concert tickets from Lara. It had been a good night.

⌘

This had been a fun Christmas for Kate. She decorated her new house for their first Christmas there and then invited us all over for the Benson Christmas Eve. We gathered early in the evening for soup and bread. I made Italian sausage and potato soup, Kate made chicken noodle soup with homemade noodles, and Nicole brought seafood chowder. Mom made all the rolls. After eating a full bowl of each kind of soup, I was stuffed. We piled in two cars and drove to a park overlooking the water where we watched a parade of boats decked out with Christmas lights. I rode over with Sam, Kate, and Izzy, who kept us entertained with "We Wish You a Merry Christmas" and her version of "Deck the Halls." We parked the cars and walked to some picnic tables with an unobstructed view.

"So, we've got to talk," Kate said. She linked her arm through mine as we walked to the tables.

"Really?" I asked. "What about?"

"You know what I'm talking about. I want to know what's going on."

I sighed. "I promise I'd tell you if I knew."

"Well, just plan on staying when everyone leaves tonight. You can help me wrap a few presents and fill me in." She let go of my arm and walked over to Sam and Izzy, giving me no chance to protest.

The lights were pretty, but watching Izzy watch the lights was even more fun. When the parade was over, we drove through a few festively lit neighborhoods before we returned to Sam and Kate's for apple pie, ice cream, and the scriptural story of the birth of the Savior. While Dad read, I looked around the room at the family I loved so much. The room was warm and cozy with just the flickering of the fireplace, the twinkling Christmas tree lights, and a lamp beside Dad. Mom sat close beside him reading silently as he read aloud. Evan and Nicole sat on the floor by the fireplace. They were holding hands. On one end of the couch, Sam was holding Izzy, with one arm around Kate, who sat next to him.

An ache started in the pit of my stomach and moved slowly to my throat. I blinked hard to hold back the stinging tears. I sat in the only single chair in the room. Single me. Me, who should have been sitting here with Dane. Oh, I wanted him here with me. I wanted his arm around me. I wanted to see the crinkles around his eyes. I wanted to give him a Christmas present. I wanted to eat pie with him. I didn't want to be here, surrounded by my family, yet so alone. I ached to be with him again.

Dad finished reading and Kate put on some soft Christmas music. Everyone talked and shared Christmas memories. Everyone but me. I sat silently, lost in my thoughts, staring into the fireplace. Suddenly, Karen Carpenter was softly singing. *Merry Christmas, Darling. We're apart it's true. But I can dream, and in my dreams, I'm Christmasing with you."* I laughed out loud. The song was so sad and cheesy and so fitting.

"What's so funny?" Dad asked. I looked up and realized everyone was looking at me.

"Nothing really," I said, shaking my head. "I'm just in a strange mood." No one pressed me for a better explanation. I was glad.

By 10:30 everyone was gone, and Sam had excused himself to put Izzy to bed. Kate pulled out some wrapping paper and a few gifts, and we got to work. "So spill it," Kate said.

"I'm not sure what to say." I concentrated on cutting wrapping paper to just the right size.

"Abby." Kate put her hand on my arm. "It's me here." I looked up and was surprised to see the concern and love on her face. "What's going on?" And then I couldn't stop them. The tears flowed. I sat down on one of the dining room chairs, buried my face in my hands, and wept. Kate pulled up a chair beside me and sat quietly waiting, her hand on my back. When I finally pulled myself together, I wiped the tears and turned to face her.

"Kate, I don't even know how it happened," I said. "One day I thought we were going to get married, and the next day it was over."

"Tell me exactly what happened," she said. So I did. I told her about Dane's birthday, the awkwardness with his family, the fight on the way home, his cool notes, his moving to Portland, everything.

"Abby, it isn't perfect, but I'm not sure it's fatal. It sounds like he's giving you time to work things out."

"Work what out?"

"Your life. Your bakery. Everything."

Was she taking his side? "I don't know what I'm supposed to do," I said.

"Abby, the bakery has taken over your life. That wouldn't have been a bad thing if you hadn't met Dane when you did. But the way it exploded has him scared. And you can't really blame him. He should have asked you more questions, but if he had, do you even know what your answers would have been?"

"What do you mean? You know I want to get married and have a family."

"I know you do. But are the things you're doing now making that possible?"

"So you think I'm wrong too."

"Whoa. I didn't say you were wrong. I'm just saying that the kind of growth the bakery's had has been crazy, and the way things are going would make it really hard to have a family. In fact, it's made it really hard for you to keep up with *our* family, let alone one where *you're* the wife and mom. I'm not saying the bakery is bad, but is it growing more than you really want it to and you don't know how to stop it?"

"Yes," I admitted. "I never thought it would be like this. It's exciting, but sometimes it's so overwhelming."

"And I'll bet sometimes Dane felt squeezed out by all of this?"

"Probably. But he never said that, and he was always supportive and positive and happy for me."

"That's because he's an amazing guy. The kind that's worth making sacrifices for. The bakery is great. You're so good at it, but maybe you need to scale it back a bit so there's room in your life for more than just the bakery."

It was all so clear when she said it. Why hadn't I talked to her sooner? I'd been worrying and stewing and dealing with everything alone, but I needed someone to tell me the truth, to carry the burden with me and help me gain a clearer perspective.

"So does everyone think the bakery has taken over my life?" I asked.

"Well, it kinda has, hasn't it?"

"So Dane's family was only thinking what my family was thinking?"

"We've all been a little worried," Kate said. "We just figured we'd let you work through it with Dane. None of us realized that you and Dane were struggling so much to get through it."

"What do I do now?" I asked. "We hardly speak."

"You pray. Pray to know what you should do. Heavenly Father loves you and Dane. Pray to know what he wants you to do." Kate leaned over and hugged me tightly. "And stop trying to handle things alone. We aren't meant to go through things by ourselves. That's what family is for."

"I love you, Kate. Thanks."

"I love you too." We finished wrapping presents, and then I drove to Dad and Mom's, where I stayed overnight in anticipation of Christmas morning.

Christmas was cold and snowy. Kate, Sam, and Izzy were at Sam's family's, and Evan and Nicole were with Nicole's family. Christmas with Dad and Mom was quiet and relaxed. We all slept in. Since we were saving the presents for evening, when everyone would be together, we made a big breakfast of pancakes, eggs, bacon, and toast. It didn't feel much like Christmas as we sat down together to eat.

"I didn't hear you come in last night," Mom said. "You and Kate must have been having a great time playing Santa."

"Izzy got up twice while we were wrapping the presents," I said. "I'm not sure if she was asleep or not when I left at a little after midnight."

"This is her first Christmas of understanding what's going on," Mom said.

"So are you okay, honey?" Dad asked.

"I will be," I said and smiled at him.

"We've been a little worried about you," Mom said.

"I know. Kate told me. I'm going to get things under control."

"I hope so," said Dad. "You know, a good thing isn't a good thing if it becomes too much to carry. It feels a little like your life has been hijacked the last few months."

"I know. I'm really glad the bakery is successful, but I'm afraid of what it's doing to my life. I have to figure out how to rein it in a little."

"You know, I've always tried not to be too nosy when it comes to dating and such," Mom said, "but whatever has happened with Dane seems to have left you a little out of sorts. You'll let us know if there's anything we can do, right?"

"I will, Mom. Thanks. I'm hoping things are going to be okay when he comes back."

"If that's what's best, then we hope so too." Dad reached over and squeezed my hand.

Later that day, Dad watched television, flipping through a few sports and part of a movie while Mom and I put together a giant jigsaw puzzle of birds on a fence. It felt good to sit quietly and put pieces together. If only the pieces of my life could fit together this perfectly. If only it could be this easy.

The rest of the family arrived in the early evening, and we ate ham and all the fixings. Only Mom and Dad and I were hungry since everyone else was on their second dinner of the day. After we ate, we gathered in the living room and exchanged Christmas gifts. It was a lovely evening. My favorite part was watching Izzy open the Fancy Nancy doll and dress up clothes I'd given her. She insisted that Kate dress her up immediately, and then she danced around the room, blissfully content as only a three-year-old can be.

Thirty-two

BLAT Sandwich

whole grain bread
mayonnaise
bacon
lettuce
avocado (sliced thinly)
tomatoes
butter

*Fill two slices of bread with all ingredients except butter.
Lightly butter the outside of the bread and grill until golden
on each side.*

The week between Christmas and New Year's was the busiest week
since the bakery had opened. Starting with December 26, we had
at least two cakes every day until January 2. I couldn't imagine wanting
to share your wedding day with New Year's Eve, but we had two cakes
on that day as well. In all, we had nineteen cakes in eight days. Every
day we arrived at the bakery in the wee hours of the morning and finally
went home to crash for a few hours late each night. I knew this was a
pace we couldn't keep up, and I looked forward to things slowing down
a bit after this crazy week was over.

Lara and April had dates on New Year's Eve, so I offered to make both deliveries so they could go home and get ready for their dates. I wasn't just being nice. I wanted to stay busy so I'd have less time to think about the fact that I didn't have anyone to ring in the New Year with.

The second delivery was to The Canal, a gorgeous waterfront reception center decorated with more crystal and twinkling lights than I'd ever seen in one place. It was like entering a fairy tale, and the wedding cake fit right into the surroundings. It was a sparkling, icy-blue fondant with dozens of tiny, crystal snowflakes scattered across the surface. The glistening snowflakes reflected the lights throughout the room. I doubted that pictures could do it justice, but I snapped a few before leaving.

The freezing air bit my face as I left The Canal, and I cranked the heat in the van as I drove home. I was bone tired and knew that tomorrow, when most of the world was taking the day off, we'd be back at the bakery working hard. Not since I was a little girl had I been asleep when the New Year arrived, but tonight, I was looking forward to being asleep a couple of hours before it made its appearance.

My phone played a funny little jingle, indicating I had a message, so I picked it up and hit the message button. A moment later, I heard Dane's voice.

"Hi, Abby. Just calling to wish you a Happy New Year. My uncle's neighbors invited us over for a party, so I wanted to give you a call before we leave. If you get this in the next half hour, give me a call. See ya."

I quickly looked to see if it had been a half an hour yet. I had about five minutes, so I hit the call button.

"Hello?"

"Hi. It's Abby."

"I can tell," he said, and we laughed together. That hadn't happened for such a long time.

"I just got your message."

"I was hoping you'd call."

"So you're going to a party?" I asked.

"Yeah, the neighbors invited us over. I guess we'll play some board games and eat and watch the ball drop."

"Sounds like fun."

"You got any big plans tonight?" he asked. Was he just being polite? I hoped not.

"Huge plans. I'm going home right now, making myself a peanut butter sandwich to celebrate, and going to bed."

"Sounds exciting."

"After this week, you have no idea how exciting it sounds."

"Busy week, huh?" Why had I said something that would remind him of the craziness of the bakery?

"Pretty busy. For some reason, half of Seattle decided to get married between Christmas and New Year's. I delivered two cakes tonight. I think it's a crazy night to get married."

"It'll be pretty hard for them to forget their anniversary," Dane said.

"That's true. I didn't think of that little upside."

I heard some voices in the background. "I'll be right there," Dane said. "Just give me a minute. Sorry. They're getting ready to go."

"Okay," I said. It was hard to hide my disappointment. We had felt almost like our old selves, and I didn't want to say good-bye.

"I'm glad you called me back," Dane said.

"Me too. Have fun tonight."

"Thanks. Good-bye."

"Good-bye."

When I got home, I skipped the sandwich and ate a piece of toast and a cup of hot cocoa. I replayed the entire conversation in my mind and planned to do that again before I fell asleep. Unfortunately, I don't think I made it past the first hello before I had drifted off.

January 3 was Sunday. It was also the first day in nine that we hadn't had multiple wedding cakes to make and deliver. After church, I drove to Dad and Mom's house. Since they had church later in the day, dinner would be in the evening, but I needed some peace and quiet away from the bakery. I needed to be able to move and think without seeing the bakery through my front window.

I let myself in with the key Mom kept hidden in the fake rock by her pink rosebush. Once inside I walked straight to the room that had once been my bedroom. It still felt like my room. Mom had taken down a few posters, and the closet was now filled with her quilting fabric, but other than that, it looked and felt the same.

I sat on the bed and ran my hands over the knobby bumps of the pink chenille bedspread. As I looked around the room, my eyes stopped on the empty bulletin board that was hanging on the wall above my desk. During my teenage years, the bulletin board had been filled with scriptures and Young Women's handouts. That was the bulletin board that had held my future children's names as well as a list of the qualities I was looking for in a future husband, another of my mementos from an especially good Young Women's lesson. Even though they were gone, I could still see them hanging there in my mind's eye.

Ian
Grant
Jane
Alice
Eliza

These were the names I'd loved for so many years.

A strong testimony
Kind
Hard-working
Good sense of humor
Handsome

The qualities I wanted in a husband.

The first list was still way in the future. The second list had been within my reach. I slid off the bed and onto my knees and began to pray. Fervent, desperate prayer. I told Heavenly Father I loved Dane and didn't want to lose him. I needed him. I asked Heavenly Father to help me know what I needed to do to be worthy of the blessings I wanted. I told Him I was thankful for the success of my bakery, and I expressed my fear of failure. And I needed help. I needed help to be able to balance my life so I could have the things that were worth the most. Tears fell freely as I unloaded the burdens I had been carrying.

I stretched out on my bed and thought about my life. I *was* too busy. I was completely exhausted and overwhelmed. I loved making beautiful cakes, and I loved working with Lara and April and Kelly, but I realized that for the past couple of months, my feelings had changed. My priorities had slowly shifted without me even realizing it. I thought about how many days had passed without me opening my scriptures, about how many Sundays I had delivered wedding cakes, about how many nights my prayers had been short and trivial as I hurried through them to get a few more minutes of sleep. How had I let these things happen?

And then I realized what a blessing I had been given when I met Dane—strong, hard-working, kind, handsome, and good Dane. He was a man I knew would lead a family righteously and provide for them. He would love his children and cherish his wife. He would make time for fun and would teach with love. He was everything I had ever wanted in a husband.

Suddenly I wanted to make my New Year's resolutions. I walked to my old desk and was glad to find a notebook and pen in the top drawer. I sat down on the bed with my back against the wall and wrote my first resolution.

1. Get Dane back.

And then I had a realization, and I crossed that out. If I had any hope of getting Dane back, I needed to be worthy of getting him back. There it was again. Worthy. Worth. I had to be worth having. How many times in Young Women's had I heard, "If you want to *find* the right one, you have to *be* the right one"? I needed to make a few changes. So I started my list over.

Pray more earnestly.
Read my scriptures every day.
No more cakes on Sundays. Ever.
Adjust the bakery so that my schedule allows me to have balance in my life.

I knew the last one would be especially hard, but I knew I needed to do it. I wanted it to be a wonderful bakery, a successful bakery, a bakery that would provide good jobs for me and my three employees. But I also wanted it to be a happy place, a comfortable place, a place where all of us could have good jobs and still have good lives. I wanted to make Aunt Grace proud. But more than that, I wanted to make my Heavenly Father proud.

"Abby?" Mom said. "Are you here?"

"I'm in here, Mom." I closed the notebook and put it in my bag. I stepped out into the hallway and met Dad and Mom who were just getting home from church.

"I'll get changed and then we can start dinner," she said.

"Sounds great. I'll help," I said. I felt freer and happier than I had in a long time.

For the next couple of days, I made lists and wrote down ideas for how to make the bakery more manageable. I didn't want to put Lara and April and Kelly in a difficult situation, but I knew that I was supposed to make some changes in my life to be ready for a good marriage and a happy family. I knew that was more important than the bakery. How to manage the goals I had set weighed on my mind as I worked and filled my thoughts every evening at home. It became a major part of my prayers, and over the next several days, I began to form a plan that made sense. Ideas came to my mind that felt inspired. I was excited.

One day when we didn't have a cake, I asked everyone to gather for a meeting. We sat in the showroom, Kelly and April on the couch and Lara on the other chair beside me. I pulled out my notes and began.

"First of all, I don't want anyone to be alarmed. This meeting is to share some ideas I've had, and I want everyone's feedback. It has been one year since I found out I'd be able to open this bakery, less than nine months since I opened the doors. My hope was to have the bakery be a success in the next five years." Everyone smiled. "It has far exceeded any expectations I think anyone had. I am surprised and grateful for the success, but honestly, it happened so fast that I wasn't able to plan and build and prepare for that kind of growth. I wasn't even able to decide if I *wanted* the bakery to grow that much, let alone that fast."

The phone rang and Kelly started to stand. "Just let the machine pick it up," I said. I took a deep breath and exhaled slowly. "Truthfully, I don't want to be this busy. I want to have a successful bakery, but I don't want to sacrifice my entire life, or yours, to this bakery. It needs to fit our needs, not the other way around. So here are a few things I'd like to do.

"First of all, I want to do three cakes a week. That's a manageable amount of work, and I can handle that much by myself. I can handle the deliveries, and by doing three cakes a week, I think I'll still make a decent living, but I won't be giving up other things that are important to me."

There was a look of fear on all their faces. I gave them a reassuring smile. "I said not to worry. Lara and April, you've learned quickly, and you do beautiful work. I want each of you to take on the number of cakes you want to do. If I want to do three cakes per week and Lara wants to do four cakes per week and April wants to do two cakes per week, then when Kelly gets calls, she'll set up the first consultation for me, the second for Lara, the third for April, the fourth for me, the fifth for Lara, and so on. Does that make sense?" They nodded.

"Would we have to handle our own consultations?" April asked. She still looked scared.

"Eventually. For a while, I would meet with you. When you feel comfortable, you would start doing them on your own."

"What if customers are disappointed because they don't get you?" April asked.

"Most clients want the bakery, and they'll be getting the bakery. I think it will be fine. If it ends up being a problem, we'll work it out, but I don't think it will."

"So do we turn people away if you all have the number of cakes you want?" Kelly asked.

"I'm afraid so. We can't continue the pace we've kept since *The Today Show*. We'll all be sick, and we'll all want to quit."

"I *have* been pretty wiped out," Lara said. "And it felt like I didn't have any time left over for Jason or my family."

"Exactly. That's what I don't want to have. If our lives suffer because of how busy we are, then no matter how much money we're making, it isn't worth it."

"Speaking of money, how will that work?" April asked.

"I've thought a lot about that, and I think the fairest way to handle it is for each of us to get the payments for the cakes we make. I want to continue pricing the cakes the way we do now, which means some weeks, I might make a lot more than you two, but other weeks you might make a lot more than me. I think it will all average out pretty well."

"I think it sounds fair," Lara said.

"As far as the business goes, there are going to be business expenses. I've decided that right off the top, we'll each put forty percent back into the business. We'll use this fund for maintenance and repairs on the bakery and vans, advertising, cake supplies, and to pay Kelly's salary." Kelly noticeably relaxed. "I went through the books, and this seems about right to me. We'll all have to work together to support the business. If we end up with a lot left over at the end of the year, we'll all get a nice bonus."

Lara and April nodded. I could tell they liked my plan.

"Don't you want a percentage of each cake?" Lara asked. "I mean, as the owner?"

"No. If everyone is handling their own business and we're all putting money back into the bakery, I don't need more than I'll make from my own cakes. Do any of you see any problems?" They shook their heads. "Then I guess we've got a plan."

"What do we do about scheduling with the vans? How do we make sure a van is available for each delivery?" Lara asked.

"I'm buying a third van," I said. That was already on one of my to-do lists. "With a van assigned to each of us, we'll be able to handle our own deliveries. Of course, I still want us to feel like a team. I want us to help each other when we can and pick up the slack when we need to. And of course, we'll have to keep the same schedule we planned for the week of McKenzie Merriweather's wedding. April, you'll still go with me to California, and Lara, you'll still handle the cakes here that week."

"Lots of changes," Lara said. "But they're good."

"Of course the bakery is mine, but I want it to be almost like each one of us has our own little business."

"I think it's an amazing plan," Kelly said. "You must've been working on this for a while."

"I've spent a lot of time on this. I love you guys and it's important to me that this be good for all of us. If we run into any glitches along the way, we'll work them out, but I feel really good about it." They were all nodding in agreement. "I think we should get through January and February with all of us working together like we have been, but tomorrow, I'd like everyone to come in with a schedule for Kelly of the number of cakes you want to do each week. Look at the calendar and see if you can figure out when you'll want to take vacation so Kelly can leave that time open."

The meeting ended with a buzz of excitement. Everyone stayed around and talked for long enough that we ordered our favorite sandwiches from the café around the corner so we could keep talking. If everyone's enthusiasm was any indication, this plan really could work.

Thirty-three

Beef and Barley Soup

2 lbs. beef stew meat, trimmed and cut into 1-inch
  pieces
2 tsp. olive oil
2 cups chopped potatoes
2 cups chopped carrots
4 garlic cloves, minced
6 cups water
1½ tsp. salt
1 tsp. dried thyme
½ teaspoon freshly ground black pepper
4 bay leaves
2 (14-oz.) cans less-sodium beef broth
1 cup uncooked pearl barley

*Heat a large Dutch oven over medium-high heat. Coat
pan with cooking spray. Add half of beef; cook 5 minutes,
browning on all sides. Remove from pan. Repeat procedure
with remaining beef.*

*Heat oil in pan over medium-high heat. Add potato,
carrot, and garlic; sauté 4 minutes or until lightly browned.
Return beef to pan. Add rest of the ingredients (except barley);
bring to a boil. Cover, reduce heat, and simmer for 1 hour.
Add barley; cook for 30 minutes or until beef and barley are
tender. Discard bay leaves.*

꧁ꕥ꧂

From somewhere amid the piles of clothes, shoes, and suitcases, my cell phone rang. Tossing clothes aside, I finally found it under a stack of socks.

"Hello?"

"Oh, hello. I'm trying to reach Abby Benson?"

"This is Abby."

"Hi, Abby. I'm April's mom, Karen."

"Hi, Karen." Dread settled into my stomach like a stone.

"April wouldn't let them take her into surgery until I promised I'd call you."

"Surgery? Is she okay?"

"She will be. They just took her in for an emergency appendectomy. But I'm afraid her doctor says there's no way she can go to California. She said to tell you she's really sorry."

"Oh wow. I hope she's all right. Tell her to concentrate on getting better and not to worry about work. We'll get by."

"Thank you, Abby. She was so upset about leaving you in a bind."

"No, no. The important thing is that she gets well. Tell her it's covered and I'll see her when I get back."

I hung up the phone and fell in a heap onto a pile of clothes. What was I going to do? I had no one to go with me. Lara and Kelly had a full schedule of cakes in the bakery. Kate was sick and miserable with her pregnancy, and Dad and Mom were celebrating their anniversary on a ship somewhere in the Caribbean until next Sunday. I had no choice but to cover McKenzie Merriweather's wedding by myself. But how?

Bad dreams kept me awake most of the night. In the first dream, I missed my flight to California and had to walk there, pulling the wedding cake behind me in a rusted-out Radio Flyer wagon. The wheel fell off the wagon twice, and both times, the cake tumbled to the ground, destroying the icing on one side of the cake.

In the second nightmare, all four of us who worked at A Piece of Cake were side-by-side in hospital beds. When we started talking to each other, we discovered that all of us had just come out of surgery, and no one was available to do any cakes that week. Panicked, I tried to sneak out of the hospital in my blue gown, but a policeman, who was sitting in the waiting room watching a football game, said, "Doctor, she's trying to get away."

In the last dream, I had an enormous bowl of icing that I was supposed to color black. I added the black food coloring and nothing happened. I added the entire jar, and still the icing was pure white. I poured a second jar of black food coloring into the icing. It went in black, but as I mixed it, the icing turned white. The lace I was to pipe on McKenzie's cake was supposed to be black, but no matter how much color I added, the icing remained white.

After the third dream, I gave up and opened the notebook I'd used to plan out all the cakes for McKenzie's wedding. How would I ever manage this alone? There were twenty tiers of cake to make. That meant seventy layers of cake to bake. I had planned that April would do all the baking while I decorated. Now I was going to have to do both. Icy fear clutched my insides. I'd never failed to deliver a cake that had been ordered. Would my first disaster really be for a celebrity whose wedding would be splashed on the pages of magazines around the world? Would I make national headlines for the wrong reason? I could picture *The Today Show* doing a follow-up story, with Matt Lauer asking me how I single-handedly ruined the wedding of America's sweetheart.

I started to cry. And then I cried harder and harder. I couldn't pull myself together. I sobbed until I had the hiccups. This was all too much. I'd never felt so helpless. What had I done to deserve this? And then my sobs were interrupted by my own voice, and I realized I'd started praying. I begged for help, for the superhuman strength and focus I would need to fulfill this order. I felt a little better. I would have to work hard and do the best I could by myself. There was no other choice. I wiped away the tears and went to shower.

Our airline tickets had arrived by Federal Express a week earlier, along with information and confirmation numbers for a rental car and hotel rooms. Everything I'd need for the week was packed and sitting by my front door. Everything except an assistant. Lara arrived around ten. One look at me and her smile turned to concern.

"What's the matter? What's wrong?"

I told her about April, proud of myself for keeping my composure as I spoke.

"Then who's going with you?"

"It's just me." I put on a smile that I knew looked more like a grimace.

"Abby, you can't do all those cakes alone. There's no way. Can't your mom or your sister help you?"

"Neither of them can go. No one can. I'll just have to manage."

"Oh man, this is *not* good."

"Lara, I've been up most of the night trying to figure out how to do this. I'll just have to work hard and fast. And smart. There's no time for any stupid mistakes."

"Well, whatever you do, don't even think about things here. Kelly and I will take care of the bakery. You focus on your work there."

"I will. You have no idea what a relief it is to know you've got things here under control."

"Sheesh! I feel so bad for you."

"I'll get by." If only I could convince myself of that, I would feel a lot better.

"Well, let's get you loaded up," Lara said. "You sure can't afford to miss your flight. You need all the time you can get."

We loaded my bags in the van and pulled out onto the street.

"I hope you get to meet McKenzie Merriweather," Lara said at the airport. "If you do, try to get a few pictures.

"I'll do my best," I said.

"Do you think her cake will end up in a magazine?"

"At this point, I'm going to be happy to have her cake end up on the table," I said. I smiled at her worried expression. "Lara. I was trying to crack a joke." I hugged her good-bye and walked into the terminal. I felt tired already, and my week had barely begun.

It started snowing while I waited for my flight—big, lazy snowflakes that landed on the concrete and melted. Before long, they were coming down harder and sticking to the ground. This did little to ease my mind. I had no time for a delayed flight. Every minute in California was important. I felt some relief when we took off only twenty minutes late, but I couldn't relax. Sitting still on the plane wasn't getting cake supplies purchased or cakes baked, and I could only schedule out my next six days so many times. I closed my eyes, but I couldn't sleep.

We left the snow somewhere over Oregon, and when we landed, Sacramento was cold and clear. Within an hour of landing, I was on I-80 heading west to Napa Valley in my rental car. With my directions on the seat beside me, I carefully made my way to the hotel, praying I wouldn't waste time making a wrong turn.

The Mediterranean-style Embassy Suites was luxurious and comfortable. If only April were here, we'd have had time to enjoy ourselves a little. I quickly unpacked my bags and gathered the things I'd need at the kitchen. Within half an hour of checking into the hotel, I was on my way to the Culinary Institute.

Emil was a short man with a round belly and tiny spectacles. He led me through the large, stone hallways, past the auditorium-style classrooms, and to a kitchen nearly twice the size of the kitchen in my bakery. The room was filled with stainless steel, from the cabinets to the countertops to the appliances. Two large stainless steel islands stood in the center of the room. I had never had so much workspace before. "I hope this will work for you," he said.

"Is it all for me? For the whole week?"

"That's what they paid for. Oh, they also paid for your meals, as well, so I'll be bringing in lunch and dinner each day for you and your assistant."

"Oh, my assistant couldn't make it, so there will just be me."

"Very well then. I'll bring you some dinner in a few hours."

"That will be great." I ran my hand over the cool, stainless steel island.

"Lucinda said you'd be doing your own shopping for supplies. You can use the pantry and the cooler for your groceries. You should find everything you need for baking and decorating here in the kitchen, but if you can't find something you need, just give me a little holler."

"Thank you, Emil."

"Here is a key to this room. Be sure to lock up whenever you leave. No sense having curious students or tourists making their way in here to get a peek at Miss Merriweather's cake." Then he put his hand up to his mouth and whispered, "Or the paparazzi." He noticed my look of alarm and patted my arm. "Now don't you worry. We've got security here. Just dial 8 on that phone if you need anything. And if you end up needing in or out of the front doors after hours, just call security. It's a pleasure having you here."

After Emil left, I took a quick inventory of the kitchen. The next several hours were spent shopping and unloading. It was an enormous job, and by the time I'd put away the last bag of powdered sugar, I was utterly exhausted and it was dark outside. I taped my schedule to the front of a cabinet and stared at it. According to my post-April appendicitis schedule, I needed to have eight layers of cake baked before I left tonight. My arms ached, and I had a stress headache. I was hungry and tired. Should I bake the cakes and stay on schedule, or should I get a good night's sleep and start fresh in the morning?

I decided I had better bake. If I got behind, I would spend the whole week playing catch-up. Just after midnight, I called James from security. Twenty minutes after he let me out the front door, I was in my bed asleep.

Monday morning arrived much too soon. A quick shower helped wake me up, and by seven o'clock I was back in the kitchen. I mixed large batches of lemon, chocolate, and carrot cake. Throughout the day, the surfaces of the kitchen filled up with baked layers. I checked and re-checked each batch to be sure I was making the proper number of each.

Lunchtime came, and Emil brought in a large bowl of beef and barley soup and two slices of crusty sourdough bread. I managed to eat a couple of bites as I worked. It was rich and delicious, and I longed to sit down and savor it, but there was no time. I was behind, and with each passing hour, the gap between where I was and where I needed to be grew wider. I was in trouble. I worked steadily throughout the day.

At about six o'clock, Emil walked through the door carrying a plate of chicken breast and egg noodles covered in a mushroom sauce with grilled asparagus. The lovely aroma woke up my stomach with a start, and I realized I was starving. "I'm heading home now," he said. "Do you need anything before I go?"

"I think I'm fine, thanks," I said.

"Abby, Abby, Abby." He held up my barely-eaten bowl of soup. "You have to have nourishment to work this hard. You must give yourself time to eat."

"I know. I'll eat when I'm finished here."

Emil looked around the kitchen. It was apparent that I'd be here a long time. "That's not good enough. Abby, you take a break and sit down. Eat every bite of this before you go back to work. You won't get these cakes finished if you make yourself sick. I mean it."

I didn't have time to take a break and eat. I still had about thirty layers of cake to bake, and I was nervous. No, I was actually panicky. I needed to be through baking tonight, and I wouldn't make it even if I stayed up all night. And I was hungry.

"Thank you, Emil. This looks heavenly."

"I'm going now. I'll see you in the morning. Don't stay too late." At the door he turned back. "Now eat." He smiled and waved.

The food was delicious, and Emil was right—I felt better after eating.

Once again, I worked until after midnight. I was weary, and each layer felt heavier than the last. The clock moved forward much too quickly. My feet were throbbing, and I was so tired when I left, I was sure I would fall asleep immediately. But I didn't. My mind was running through the schedule again and again, trying to piece together a plan that would work. I was already so far behind. This week's work needed two people, and no matter how hard or fast I worked, I was still only me. I still had baking to do, and I needed to be filling and stacking the cakes. I still had to ice them, cover each cake with fondant, and then do hours of meticulous lacework. I hadn't had time to make or paint the three hundred black fondant buttons.

I wasn't going to make it. Anxiety gnawed at my stomach, and I felt sick. I needed a miracle.

Finally, after more than an hour of worry and prayer and even a few tears, I fell into a troubled sleep.

At eight the next morning, I walked through the stone halls of the Culinary Institute. Classes had already started in a couple of the auditoriums, and I felt jealous of the people who were sitting there learning, relaxed and unconcerned. Their careers were before them, bright and hopeful. They didn't have to worry that in less than five days their careers would be lying around them in ruins.

A man was leaning against the wall next to the door of my kitchen. A tall man. A handsome man. After a few steps, I stopped. All rational thought evaporated, and I stood there unable to speak.

"Hi," he said.

For too long I just looked at him as my mind slowly began to process what my eyes were seeing. He smiled. "How's it going?" I stepped forward and touched his arm. He was real. And he was here. This wasn't a creation of my overloaded and overwhelmed mind.

"What are you doing here?" A noisy group of students in white chef coats walked by. When they passed, I looked back at Dane. He was still there.

"I heard you might need some help."

I let out a sigh that sounded more like a gust of wind. "Really?"

"I stopped by the bakery yesterday, and Lara told me what happened to April. She was so worried about you, I realized you might be in trouble."

"You have no idea. I can't get done in time," I said. It came out as a whisper and my voice was unsteady.

"Hey, it's okay," he said. "You've got help now. Let's get in there, and you can start bossing me around."

I was shaking and emotional and had trouble getting the key in the door, but soon we were inside. The only cake Dane had ever baked was when he was fourteen and he and Blake had made a birthday cake for their mom. But he was a fast learner and a whiz at following directions. Soon, he was mixing up batter while I started putting together the cakes.

Conversation was limited to giving and receiving directions for most of the morning. Just before noon, Emil stopped by to see if I was ready for some lunch. A few minutes later, he brought back two gourmet bleu cheese hamburgers with sweet potato fries. We worked all day, and I was filled with hope as we made up ground on the schedule.

"If I'd known you were coming, I'd have kept April's room for you," I said.

"That's okay. Kelly booked me a room."

"How long are you staying?" I asked, afraid of the answer.

"When do you deliver the cakes?"

"They have to be set up by Saturday at five."

"Well, then I guess I'm staying until Saturday at six."

I looked at him to see if he was joking. He smiled, but it wasn't a teasing smile. "Do you promise?" I asked.

"Unless you don't need me. But I think maybe you do."

"You know I do. Oh, Dane. Thank you."

"Too bad I don't have cake-decorating experience. I'm not the best help you could have, but hopefully I'm better than no help at all."

"You're excellent help." I didn't know what else to say, so I turned my attention back to the cake I was filling and bit my lip.

We left at about ten that night. The baking was finished, the cakes were layered and stacked. A few of them were iced and covered with fondant. I was still a little behind my schedule, but now that I wouldn't have to do everything alone, it looked like I might make it.

"I'll see you in the morning," Dane said in the parking lot.

"Sounds good. Thanks again."

At the road, I turned to my hotel, and he turned the other direction to his.

What did this mean? We had just spent all day together, and neither of us had said anything about the past or the future. Did this mean he still loved me? Or did he just feel sorry for me?

Dane arrived just behind me on Wednesday, and we got right to work. By the time we took a break to eat lunch, all the cakes were covered in fondant. After lunch, I showed Dane how to make fondant buttons. His big hands were clumsy at first, but by the time he'd made a few, he was getting the hang of it. I sat on a stool and started piping black lace. This part couldn't be rushed. It was delicate, meticulous work.

We passed the afternoon and evening listening to music while I piped and Dane molded buttons. He didn't try to start a conversation, and I was glad. I needed to concentrate on what I was doing, and having him six feet away was distraction enough. If he had started talking, I would have found it difficult to focus on the job at hand. And even though I had so many questions, the quiet was nice. We were together, and I wondered if these days represented the beginning or the end. I didn't want to worry about that right now.

Thursday was more of the same. I decorated cakes, and Dane finished molding the buttons. When they were all molded, I showed him how to mix the black coloring with lemon extract to create an edible paint. Starting with the buttons he had molded, he began to paint. Conversation was sporadic. We would have a conversation about a song on the radio and then silence for an hour. We talked about a couple of movies we had seen while we were apart. The breaks were long, but not uncomfortable. It was so easy to be together. Oh, how I had missed him.

Friday morning I continued piping lace. My hand was tired, and I had to stop once in a while to shake out the cramping muscles. The buttons were finished, so I showed Dane how to roll out a long rope of fondant and then roll a piece of grosgrain ribbon onto it to transfer the texture of the ribbon onto the fondant before painting it black. Then I showed him how to apply it to the bottom of each cake and how to attach the buttons up the back of the cake.

He finished the cakes as I completed my part. When he had to wait on me, he washed the pans and cleaned the kitchen. By evening, the kitchen was put back together, and most of the cakes were in the cooler. There were three more cakes to pipe and finish, but we were ahead of schedule, and the cakes were going to be ready.

I got to my hotel room a little before nine. My back ached from leaning over the cakes all day. I looked out my window at the steam coming off the warm, glowing pool. It was too much to resist. I pulled my hair into a ponytail, put on my suit, and went down to the pool for a swim. The warm water felt good, and I felt my tight muscles release. The water lapped against the side of the pool as I floated. I felt light and relaxed. I hadn't felt this good all week.

The phone was ringing as I walked into the room.

"Hey, Abby." It was Dane.

"Hi."

"I was flipping through the channels and *The Italian Job* is just starting on Channel 243."

"Oh, thanks. I'll turn it on."

"Maybe you're too tired to watch it, but if you're not, I think you'll like it." I turned on the television and flipped it to the right channel.

"I feel pretty good. I just went swimming, and it felt so nice to move around. And now that I know I'm going to make the deadline, how could I not feel good? Oh, I didn't know Edward Norton was in this."

"Yeah, he's pretty good. And it's got a great story. Most action movies don't have much of a story."

"Thanks for calling. I think this is exactly what I need tonight."

"No problem. You can tell me if you liked it in the morning."

"Okay. I'll see you at eight."

"Bye, Abby."

He was right. I liked the movie, and it was just the right mix of story, romance, and action. The only thing that would have made it better was if we could have watched it together.

Saturday was beautiful. The air was clear and bright. By noon the cakes were finished. Lucinda, who I hadn't seen since arriving in California, swept into the kitchen in a tailored gray suit and heels that made my feet hurt. She carried a clipboard that gave her an air of authority.

"Are the tables all set up so we can get the cakes delivered?" Lucinda asked.

"I don't know. I haven't been—"

Lucinda put up her hand to stop me from talking, and only then did I realize she had in an earpiece and she wasn't talking to me. "Good. I'll have the baker go ahead and begin delivering the cakes. There are so many of them, it's going to take her a while." She paused but continued to hold her hand up toward me. I kept quiet. "Yes, go ahead and send over the van. I'm here looking at the cakes right now, and I'm sure it's going to take two or three trips. Good. Bye for now."

Lucinda put down her hand and turned to me. "Oh, Abby, these are spectacular. McKenzie will be thrilled."

"Good. I'm glad you like them."

"Now, I have a driver on his way. You can go ahead and get these set up, and then you're free to go. I know your flight doesn't leave until nearly midnight, but hopefully you can find something to occupy yourself for a few hours in Sacramento."

"Don't worry about me. I'll be fine."

"Now, just a reminder. Ms. Merriweather has agreed that you can use photos of the cake in your portfolio and to promote your bakery, but I must remind you that you've signed a contract that you won't sell any images or information about the wedding to any publication."

"I understand." I could see Dane smiling behind Lucinda, and it was difficult not to smile with him. Who would ever have thought I would be signing privacy contracts?

"All right then. The driver will be here soon. We'll mail payment to your shop the first of next week." And with that, Lucinda clicked her way out of the kitchen and down the stone hall.

A few minutes later, Emil came through the door. "My, oh my, oh my, oh my," he said, moving among the cakes and nodding appreciatively. "If you ever want to teach a course here, you let me know."

"Thanks, Emil. And thanks for everything."

"You've done an amazing job. I'm very proud of you." He patted my hand. "And you, young man. Way to save the day. I have a feeling we might need to get you some shining armor, don't you think, Abby?" I nodded.

When the driver arrived, we loaded ten of the cakes in the delivery van. I was a nervous wreck. Driving a cake is stressful, but having someone else doing the driving is even worse. I kept looking back to see how they were holding up, and even though they looked okay, I barely took a breath the entire way there.

The wedding was held at the Sebastian Vanetti Vineyards. The driver turned left down a narrow, paved driveway. Vineyards lined both sides of the road for acres and acres. The site ahead of us took my breath away. Two hot air balloons hovered above the vineyard in the bright blue sky. Both were striped pale yellow, moss green, and wine red. Written in beautiful script lettering on one balloon was "McKenzie" and on the other balloon was "Dax." As we got closer, I could see that they were anchored to the ground by about two hundred feet of rope and tied to each other so that they stayed about twenty feet apart. For a minute, I forgot about the cake as I took in the beautiful scene.

The wedding was to take place in a small, mission-style church on the property. Before we unloaded the cakes, I took a short tour to see where to carry the cakes, and there was the church. The entire end of the chapel was filled with richly colored-stained glass windows. I could see why they'd chosen to be married just before sunset. The wall was beautiful now, but would soon be on fire with the light of the setting sun. At the end of each pew were cascading anemones and begonias. The chapel smelled wonderful.

A girl who introduced herself as Lucinda's assistant guided me into the wine caverns, where the reception would take place. The stuccoed walls of the long hall curved up onto the ceiling. The air was cool and thin like the inside of a cave. Along the walls were antique kerosene lamps that cast long and flickering shadows. The hall opened up into a gigantic domed room. Lining the walls, about halfway up, were at least a hundred wine barrels. Round tables with white cloths were scattered around the room. Each table would have one of the cakes we'd made as its centerpiece.

A table in the center of the room was prepared for the wedding cake. It was draped in ivory dupioni silk with a wide, black silk border. An enormous wrought iron chandelier hung from the high ceiling directly over the spot where the cake would sit. The cake would be visible from everywhere in the room.

Dane and I brought in the first two cakes and placed them on two of the tables. When we came back with two more, several people were setting the first two tables with crystal and silver. We continued until all the cakes were inside.

The rest of the cakes fit in the back of the van, and we made our second trip. With each cake we brought in, the room looked more beautiful. Finally, with one of us on each side, we delivered the five-tiered wedding cake. We stepped carefully so we wouldn't trip on the uneven stone floor. Once it was centered on the silver stand, I stepped back to look at it from all sides. It was stunning. I'd never made a cake more ornate. From all sides it was a feast for the eyes. The lace was delicate and even. I looked around the room. Each of the individual cakes was unique, the lace a slightly different pattern than the others. It was a sight to behold. And we'd made them all.

I was pulled from my reverie by Dane standing beside me. He was so close I could feel his arm next to mine even though they weren't touching. "What do you think?" I said.

"I think it's pretty amazing. She's gonna be blown away."

"You're thinking about a career change, aren't you?" I asked.

Dane laughed. "I don't think so."

"Look at all those buttons you made. Are you telling me you don't want to spend your life making buttons?"

"It's tempting, but I think I'll stick with building."

I took several pictures of each cake, and then we left. As the van turned onto the main road, we were passed by a procession of about twenty antique cars. "There's the wedding party," the driver told us. I craned my neck but couldn't see the bride. I watched the vintage cars for as long as I could. It was like watching another era pass by, and for some reason I felt nostalgic for things I'd lost. I didn't dare think about what all those things might be.

Thirty-four

Frangipane Torte

1 (8-oz.) can almond paste
½ cup sugar
½ cup butter, room temperature
3 eggs, room temperature
½ cup cake flour
confectioners' sugar
melted chocolate

Preheat oven to 350°F. Grease and flour a 9-inch tart pan.

Add almond paste, sugar, and butter to a mixing bowl. With mixer on low speed, combine ingredients, then beat on high for 2–3 minutes. Add eggs, one at a time, beating well between each. Beat on high until batter is pale and fluffy (about 3 minutes).

Sift cake flour into almond mixture. Gently fold in flour by turning with a spatula until ingredients are just barely mixed. Do not stir.

Spread batter into tart pan. Bake for 30 minutes or until golden and a toothpick inserted in the middle comes out clean. Cool completely on a wire rack before removing from pan. Sprinkle with confectioners' sugar and drizzle with melted chocolate.

⟨∞⟩

I was ready to go home. Now that the cake was delivered, I realized how tired I was. I had been running in overdrive for six days, and I couldn't wait to get a good night's sleep. I forced myself to put Dane and what this week meant out of my mind. If it didn't mean anything to him, I didn't want to get my hopes up. I was too tired to think rationally anyway.

I checked out of the hotel, and two hours later I ate a ham-and-cheese bagel at the airport. I already missed Dane and wished he'd been on the same flight home as me. Now, with three hours to wait until my flight, I had plenty of time to think about the week. I replayed each day since Dane had arrived. He'd been friendly but reserved, maybe even a little distant. He had never made an effort to touch me, and our conversations, while pleasant enough, never got personal. He hadn't said a single thing about seeing each other when we got back to Seattle.

But he had come all this way to help me. That had to mean something, didn't it? Would he do that if he didn't still love me? Or at least care a little bit? I was so confused, and the only person who could help me sort through it all was Dane.

⟨∞⟩

The next week was just a regular week at the bakery, and I loved it. We weren't overly busy, there were no television interviews, and I didn't make a cake for a celebrity. I was able to go home on time each day, and I didn't have flowers or bows to make in the evening. I read a book, visited Dad and Mom, and even watched a little television. I felt more normal than I had in weeks.

"It's here," Kelly said at my office door. She was holding an envelope, and I knew what it must be. We'd been speculating when it would come and how much it would be. I knew Dane and I had delivered beautiful cakes to McKenzie Merriweather's wedding, but people who are used to having whatever they want are sometimes hard to please. I hoped it was good news.

I took the envelope, and we gathered in the kitchen. "Let's have a look at this," I said. I opened the card and avoided looking at the check until after I read the card.

Dear Abby,

McKenzie loved, loved, loved the cakes. She was speechless when she saw them. She asked me to tell you what a beautiful job you did.

I'd love to call on you again in the future if I have clients in the market for something as magnificent as that. You are a master at your craft. I've enclosed your payment.

Thank you for being such a dream to work with.

Lucinda

"How much is it?" asked Lara.

I turned the check over in my hand and nearly choked. The check was made out for twenty-five thousand dollars. And that was in addition to the flights, the rental car, hotel rooms, and the Culinary Institute. They'd also paid for Emil and supplies. "They can't be serious," I said.

Lara was looking over my shoulder. "I'm not surprised. The cakes were gorgeous, and there were fifteen cakes besides the wedding cake."

"I know, but usually I pay for the ingredients, and they paid for everything."

"I guess that means she was a satisfied customer," Kelly said.

"I guess so," I said.

"How much are you going to pay Dane?" Lara asked.

"I've got to figure that out."

That night Dane called. "I was thinking we should go to dinner on Saturday."

"You were?" I said.

"Well, if we can work together for a week, we should be able to sit down and eat dinner together, right?"

"Right. And I've got something for you too."

"You do? What is it?"

"I'll just wait and give it to you on Saturday."

"All right. I'll try to wait that long."

We arranged the time and hung up.

I was ready for dinner a full hour before Dane arrived. Every nerve was on end. Even though we'd spent hours together last week, this was our first date in three months. This had to be good, right? I'd taken a long, hot bath, but I still didn't feel calm. I tried to distract myself with a book, but after a while, I realized I didn't even know what I was reading, so I gave up.

Finally, Dane knocked on the door. Oh, he was handsome. He'd had a haircut this week, and although it may have meant nothing, I decided that was a good sign.

"I didn't realize we had a dress code," he said. We were both in jeans, white shirts, and sweaters. His was a navy pullover and mine was a gray cardigan, but we laughed and I felt more relaxed.

On the way, I was glad we were able to talk comfortably, although we didn't talk about the things I wanted to talk about—love, marriage, children, and kissing. Someone listening in would have been surprised that we'd known each other for more than a year. It seemed more like we'd just met. I missed holding his hand and smiling at each other easily. I wondered if he felt as awkward as I did, and I worried that we might never be comfortable with each other again.

"Where are we going?" I asked.

"I made us a reservation at Ray's Boathouse."

"Ooh, I've always wanted to eat there. I hear they have amazing seafood."

At the restaurant, we were seated by a floor-to-ceiling window that made me feel like we were sitting right on the water. Lights from the boats on the water twinkled like stars. "This is really beautiful," I said.

"Look at the Cascades." Dane pointed at the mountain range that made a jagged silhouette against the darkening sky in the distance.

"Napa Valley is beautiful, but I'll take this any day."

For the next hour, we ordered and ate and talked about Napa Valley, Portland, home restoration, celebrities, and good food. My butter-roasted halibut was rich and delicious. It felt so right to be sitting here together, and I hoped he felt that way too. We shared a piece of almond frangipane torte with chocolate sauce. We ate slowly, extending dinner as long as we dared. We were finished, and the waiter—who had checked on us three times—was growing impatient, so we reluctantly gave up our table.

Dane helped me with my coat but still didn't take my hand. I wished I had the courage to reach for his hand, but my insecurities held me back. We walked to his car with a sad, safe distance between us.

I wanted the evening to continue, but Dane drove straight to my house, and long before I wanted to be, I was alone, and Dane was driving home.

I was filled with confusion. We had had a pleasant and comfortable evening, but something seemed wrong. There had been no talk of another date. Even when we spoke briefly of Evan's upcoming wedding, there had been no promise of seeing each other. I felt sad and disappointed. I had hoped that an evening together would bring back everything we'd shared. I had wanted us to profess our love for each other and share a long, breathless kiss good night. I wanted to plan our future lives together. But it was barely 9:30, and I was alone with no promise of a future date, let alone a future life together. Maybe the changes I was making in my life and in the bakery weren't going to matter as far as Dane was concerned. I went to bed and tried to fall asleep. I wanted slumber to rescue me from the dreary thoughts that filled my mind, but after nearly an hour, I was no closer to sleep than I'd been when I first climbed under the covers.

I got up and wandered into the kitchen. I made a cup of hot cocoa and scavenged through the cupboards for a cookie or a muffin. I had to settle for a graham cracker. I sat at the counter and went through the mail. At the bottom of the stack, under grocery store coupons and credit card offers, I found the *Ensign*. I flipped through the pages. About halfway through, I came to an article called "Seek Ye First the Kingdom of God." I moved to the couch and started to read.

When I finished, I felt better. I knew the changes I was making were showing my Father in Heaven that I was putting his kingdom first. Of course, I wanted the end result to be that I got Dane, too, but if I didn't, I would try to trust Heavenly Father to know what was best. I went to bed and slept well the rest of the night.

Sunday was a beautiful day. The sky was clear, and instead of the watery, cold sun of winter, it shone strong and warm. After church was over, I considered driving out to Dad and Mom's. It wasn't the family dinner, but my house was pitifully low on food, and I really didn't feel like hanging out alone all afternoon. I changed into comfortable sweatpants and a long-sleeved T-shirt. I was putting my hair up in a ponytail when I heard a knock at the front door. I looked out the window and was surprised to see Dane.

"Hey, do you want to go for a drive?" he asked as soon as I opened the door.

"Sure. Let me change," I said. I was very underdressed next to his Sunday suit.

"No, you're fine. I just came straight from church, but I was going to stop and change at my house anyway."

I grabbed a hooded sweatshirt. "What's up?" I asked when we were driving down the street.

"I just think we need to talk."

"Oh. Okay."

But then we didn't talk. The silence drenched the air as neither of us spoke.

"Do you want to come in and make a couple of sandwiches while I change?" Dane asked in his driveway.

"Sure." While Dane changed into jeans and a sweatshirt, I made sandwiches. He took a couple bottles of water out of the fridge as we left.

I didn't know what to say as Dane drove, so I waited. A short time later, he pulled into the parking lot at the Burke Gilman trail, and we got out. Dane handed me the bag with sandwiches and water, and he got a quilt out of the backseat.

"I thought we could walk down by the water and talk," Dane said.

"All right. How was church today?" I asked. I was tired of waiting for a conversation.

"It was good. How was yours?"

"It was fine."

So much for conversation. We started walking. What was going on? I was hoping that this meant something good, but Dane seemed so absorbed in his own thoughts and with no real conversation, it scared me. Perhaps Dane just wanted closure so he could move on without guilt. Maybe he'd met someone in Portland and the only thing standing between them was making the end with me official.

We left the trail and made our way down a rough and overgrown hill to the sandy shore. Dane reached up and took my hand, helping me down the hill, but as soon as we were on smooth ground, he let go. I already missed the feel of his hand, and I felt like crying.

Yellow-and-red canoes lined the water in front of a small rental hut. A single, red canoe drifted far out in the water. The beach was mostly deserted. Only a father and child tossed a Frisbee a hundred yards away. Not too far from the canoes were a few logs scattered at haphazard angles, bleached white by the sun and salt and weather. We sat down on one of them and looked out at the water. It was quiet for so long, I wondered if Dane would ever say what he wanted to say.

He took a deep breath. I could barely breathe.

"Abby," he said and turned toward me, "I did things all wrong. I wanted to know how you felt about family and marriage and kids, and I should have just asked you. But when your bakery took off, I was afraid of what your answers would be." He looked back at the water. "And I didn't want to lose you."

"Why did you think you'd lose me?"

"Because there are certain things I can't compromise. I want to marry someone whose number one priority is our family. When the bakery took off, I was afraid you couldn't or wouldn't be able to put a family first. And if you couldn't, I'd have to go on without you." He paused. "I was afraid I'd end up losing you."

I smiled.

"What?" he asked. "What are you thinking?"

"I'm thinking I want to start over. Right now. We should ask each other whatever we've been afraid to ask. With no fear."

He looked skeptical.

"I'm serious. Ask me a question you were afraid to ask."

"Okay. Do you want kids?"

"Absolutely I do," I said. "I've always wanted kids. I've had five names picked out since I was a kid."

"Really?"

"It's true."

"What are the names?" he asked.

"Ian, Grant, Jane, Alice, and Eliza."

"Hmm. I'm not sure about Alice. Maybe we could swap that one out for David."

"I think that would depend on whether it was a boy or a girl," I said, and we laughed. "Next question."

"No, it's your turn."

"Okay." I thought for a moment. "What kind of father do you want to be?"

"The kind that takes my family to church, coaches my kids' teams, and adores my kids' mom."

"That's a good answer," I said. "Your turn."

"How will you balance a family and your bakery?" He was serious again, and I knew this was his biggest worry.

"First let me tell you about my New Year's resolutions." I told Dane about the day I'd felt overwhelmed and had been at my parents' house alone. I told him how I'd prayed for help about how to manage the bakery and get my life under control. I left out the part about wanting to get Dane back. I thought that might be a little more information than he needed at the moment. I told him about my ideas for the future of the bakery.

"Wow, Abby. I had no idea you'd even realized how crazy things were."

"Dane, you were right to worry. Things got so out of control. The bakery took on a life of its own, and I was overwhelmed and didn't know how to keep it from taking over my life. It was insane, and I'm pretty sure that wasn't what Aunt Grace had in mind. If I'd let things keep going the way they were, I would have ended up with no life, except the bakery. That isn't what I want, and I don't think that's what Aunt Grace or Heavenly Father want either. I'm sorry I got so angry at you and your family. My family was having the same concerns, and I was so buried in it all that I couldn't see straight. But I do now. Things are going to be different."

And then Dane pulled me into his arms and held me tightly. I thought he might say something, but he didn't. He just held me close. Oh, I'd missed this place. After a while, he pulled away and took my hands in his. "Do you have any more questions?" he asked.

"I don't think so," I said. "Do you?"

"Just one."

"Okay." What else could he be worried about?

"Do you still love me?" His eyes were studying my face.

"Yes," I said. He leaned over and sweetly kissed me. I melted into his arms. I'd been waiting so long for this kiss. I didn't want it to end, but too soon, he pulled back again.

"Then will you marry me?"

"Definitely, yes," I said. Dane took hold of both sides of my hooded sweatshirt and pulled me to him for another kiss. I'm not sure if it was the kiss or the question or both, but I felt like I was drowning in the best possible way.

He pulled a little box out of his pocket and handed it to me. "I got this for you back in October," he said. I opened the blue box. Inside was a platinum filigree ring with a square diamond.

"Oh, Dane, it's gorgeous." He took the ring out of the box and put it on my finger.

"I just didn't think I'd wait this long to give it to you," he said.

"When had you planned to give it to me?" I asked.

"Oh, I don't know," he said.

"Really? You didn't know when you were going to do it?"

"Well, I'd picked a time, but then that changed."

"Come on, tell me," I said.

"I was going to give it to you on my birthday," he said.

Thoughts of that awful night came to mind, and I felt ashamed and embarrassed. "Oh, Dane. I was so terrible. I feel so bad."

"That's why I wasn't going to tell you. I don't want you to feel bad. Things happen for a reason. I think we were supposed to have time to figure out what we both want and how to get it. I think the time is right now. This is how it's supposed to be." He pulled me into his arms again.

"I love you, Dane. So, so much. I'm glad you didn't give up on me."

"I couldn't give up on you. I love you too much."

Back in the car, we held hands. I couldn't stop smiling. "Hey," he said. "Didn't you say you had something you were going to give me last night?"

"Oh, I completely forgot." I reached into my purse and pulled out an envelope. Inside the envelope was a check made out to Dane.

"What's this?" he asked.

"Your payment for helping me last week."

"I never expected you to pay me."

"I know. But you earned it."

Dane pulled the car to the curb and opened the envelope. "Ten thousand dollars?" he asked. I nodded. "No way. I can't take this."

"Oh yes, you can. You were worth at least that much. I wouldn't have made it without you. Take it."

"I have a better idea." He leaned over and kissed me. "Let's use it for a wedding and honeymoon."

"I guess I can agree to that." He kissed me again and I lost all track of time.

Epilogue

Recipe for a Happy Marriage

1 boy (preferably tall and handsome with eyes that
    crinkle when he smiles)
1 girl (with unruly hair and a smattering of freckles)
similar priorities
love
kisses (lots and lots of kisses)
a gorgeous ring

Combine all ingredients and watch the magic happen.

*E*van and Nicole were married the first week of February. It was a
lovely wedding, and Nicole looked like a movie star. She was stunning in her simple white dress. When you have a face like hers, you can
understate everything else. They're very happy and just had a baby girl
last month. They named her Amelia. She has Nicole's dark hair and is
already stealing hearts.

A month after Dane and I were married, Kate and Sam welcomed
Olivia into their family. She's a much calmer child than Izzy, peaceful
and serene. Izzy loved her from the beginning and is excited that she's
now old enough to dress her up.

A Piece of Cake is thriving. I've kept to my plan, and I only do
three cakes a week. Lara and Jason got married last fall, and Lara does

five or six cakes a week. She's busy, but she's supporting them while Jason gets through law school. April only does one cake a week. She's in school full-time. She's getting a degree in accounting. I'll probably hire her to do the books when she's finished. Kelly is still with us and says she has the best job in the world. I'm glad she feels that way. We're all pretty happy there.

McKenzie Merriweather's wedding was featured in *InStyle* magazine's wedding edition. There were four pictures of my cakes. My name and the name of the bakery were captioned under two of the pictures, which brought on a tidal wave of calls. We firmly stuck to our schedule, however, and the only significant change was that the worth of our cakes rose dramatically.

A month after the magazine feature, Food Network contacted me to see if I could participate in a wedding cake challenge with a nature theme. Lara and I blocked out an entire week, and we brought our husbands with us to New York. There we experienced two stressful days of competition and three wonderful days of sightseeing. Lara and I did a larger version of the cake made with leaves and grapes. It was pretty spectacular. We didn't win, but we placed second, and once again, we were deluged with calls.

Dane was hired to help with the restoration of an old Victorian home in Poulsbo. Someone from the Historical Society stopped by to take a look one day and was so impressed by the work he was doing that Dane was hired to head up the restoration of several older homes in the historic Pioneer Square district of Seattle. That will keep him busy for the next few years.

Today I'm working on a beach-themed wedding cake that I'll deliver to Ocean Shores tomorrow. Dane just dropped off a few construction supplies. He's going to do some work on my office to make it function as both an office and a nursery. This will be the last cake I do for a few months, as our baby boy is due in three weeks. We live in the gorgeous craftsman home that Dane restored, but a few things have changed there. It no longer looks like a man's house. Now it looks like it belongs to a family. A family that is about to use one of the five or six names we have picked out. A family worth more than any bakery.

Acknowledgments

$\mathcal{L}$ike the credits in a movie, the acknowledgments page gives credit to the many wonderful people who helped make this book possible. The credits can be long and boring, but they usually have some good music to make them worth sticking around to read the names of every gaffer and boom operator. So put on your favorite song while you read through these credits.

Acquisitions Editor: Jennifer, who was a joy to work with.

Cover Art: Erica, who designed a delicious cover.

Editor: Melissa, who helped make this book better.

First Readers: Veronica, Savannah, Lori, and Mom and Dad, who read numerous drafts and gave helpful suggestions.

Leading Encouragers: My wonderful, immediate family—Travis, Bruce, Veronica, Savannah and Joseph—the best cheerleaders ever.

Encouragers in a supporting role: My big, wonderful, extended family—Lynn and Karen, Renae and Dale, Terry and Wanda, Richard and Kara, Nairn and Maria, Robert and Teresa, Lori and Scott, John and Tawnie, Lisa and John, Leslie, Spencer and Kristi, Mark and Suzy, and all my cute nieces and nephews.

Caterers: Travis and Veronica and Savannah, for taking care of dinner when I was too involved in writing to cook.

Critics: The ones who like me and say nice things and the ones I'm still trying to win over.

Best Pet: Pepper, the Great Dane, who sleeps at my feet while I write.

Readers: You, who spend your time and money to read my book. I'm grateful.

Discussion Questions

1. For many years Abby had dreamed of owning her own wedding cake shop, but when she had the opportunity to fulfill that dream, she wasn't sure if she should go for it. What do you think was holding her back? What gave her the courage to jump in?

2. What role did Abby's family play in her success? How important do you think it is to surround yourself with people who are supportive and encouraging?

3. Did you understand Abby's dilemma as she tried to figure out what to charge for her cakes? What did you think of her idea? Would you like to determine what you pay or would you prefer to have the price given to you?

4. Did you think Dane's concerns were fair? How did you feel about the way he handled Abby's success?

5. What did you think of the arrangement Abby made with her employees? Would you prefer to be paid based on what customers pay or would you prefer to be paid a set amount?

6. The success of Abby's bakery seemed to have a life of its own, and it seemed that Abby didn't know how to take control of what was happening. Have you ever been in a similar situation and felt like something else had control of your life instead of you having the control? What do you think about the changes Abby made to regain control of her life and the bakery?

7. Abby almost lost one dream as she wildly pursued another. Do you think she'd have been happy if she'd abandoned the dream of marriage to Dane and a family? Do you think she could have been happy abandoning the bakery? What can Abby's experiences teach us about priorities and balance?

About the Author

*K*arey White grew up in Utah, Idaho, Oregon, and Missouri. She attended Ricks College and Brigham Young University. Her first novel, *Gifted*, was a Whitney Award Finalist.

She loves to travel, read, bake treats, and spend time with family and friends. She and her husband are the parents of four great children. She teaches summer creative writing courses to young people and is currently working on her next book. Find out more about Karey at www.kareywhite.com.